By Faith, Not by Sight

By Faith, Not by Sight

PAUL AND THE ORDER OF SALVATION

Second Edition

RICHARD B. GAFFIN JR.

P U B L I S H I N G

P.O. BOX 817 • PHILLIPSBURG • NEW JERSEY 08865-0817

Library of Congress Cataloging-in-Publication Data

Gaffin, Richard B.
  By faith, not by sight : Paul and the order of salvation / Richard B. Gaffin, Jr. -- Second Edition.
    pages cm
  Includes bibliographical references and index.
  ISBN 978-1-59638-443-9 (pbk.)
    1. Salvation--Biblical teaching. 2. Bible. Epistles of Paul--Theology. 3. Eschatology--Biblical teaching.
  I. Title.
  BS2655.S25G34 2013
  234--dc23
                    2013030938

Contents

FOREWORD   vii

PREFACE TO THE FIRST EDITION   xv

PREFACE TO THE SECOND EDITION   xvii

1. THE ORDER OF SALVATION AND THE THEOLOGY
OF PAUL   1

    The Study of Paul Today   1

    Paul as Theologian—Some Foundations   5

      Biblical Theology and Redemptive-Historical

      Interpretation   6

      The Problem of Interpreting Paul   10

      Paul as a Theologian   14

      Biblical Theology and Systematic Theology   17

2. THE ORDER OF SALVATION AND THE "CENTER"
OF PAUL'S THEOLOGY   21

    The "Center" of Paul's Theology   23

      1 Corinthians 15:3–4   26

      Sin   34

      Union with Christ   40

      Union and Justification   45

      The Role of Faith   47

CONTENTS

The Center of Paul's Theology and the Order
of Salvation   49

    Justification in the Order of Salvation   50

3. THE ORDER OF SALVATION AND ESCHATOLOGY—1   61

Eschatology and Anthropology   61

Eschatology and Sanctification   67

    Union with Christ and the Resurrection   67

    Indicative and Imperative   77

    Historical and Theological Reflections   85

4. THE ORDER OF SALVATION AND ESCHATOLOGY—2   91

Eschatology and Justification   91

Initial Considerations   91

    The Perspective of the Westminster Standards   93

    Justification as Future   95

    Faith and Obedience   114

    Paul and James   118

    Justification and the Present   120

EPILOGUE   123

BIBLIOGRAPHY   127

INDEX OF SCRIPTURE   131

INDEX OF SUBJECTS AND NAMES   137

Foreword

IT IS A UNIQUE PRIVILEGE and a remarkable providence
to write a foreword for a book that has been so deeply influential
in my own theological thinking. Some time ago I suggested to a
group of ministers that we read *"By Faith, Not by Sight"* (Paternoster, 2006), by Richard Gaffin. When I subsequently learned that
this important volume had already gone out of print, I was disap-
pointed. But when Professor Gaffin asked me to write a foreword
for its reprinting by P&R Publishing, I was deeply honored—but
also a little surprised. After all, what could I possibly say that is
not already said better in this book? Coupled with the fact that
the Reformed world is already filled with enough sycophants—
please excuse the previous sentence!—this leaves me in a difficult
position in writing a suitable foreword to this work.

As I read this book for the first time, it occurred to me that
extensive references to early modern Reformed divines (*ca.* 1500–
1800) were absent. This is not a criticism, of course, but simply
an observation. Yet the theology expressed in the book is very
much in line with the best Reformed thinkers of that period.
Thus, a historical-theological perspective may fit nicely with
what one finds in this book—a work that highlights Professor
Gaffin's abilities as an exegete and a biblical theologian. Systematic theology should generally try to incorporate careful exegesis
and biblical theology, so I am happy to provide some historical
background, especially when some have questioned Professor
Gaffin's theology in relation to the early modern period.

The Reformed tradition has always had its opponents,
whether those who are sometimes in error (e.g., the Lutherans)

or those who are fully heretical (e.g., the Socinians). But our tradition has also had its own intra-Reformed controversies due to the fact that otherwise impeccable Reformed theologians have held views that, for example, sometimes have more in common with Lutheran or antinomian theology. This book deals with a number of the more sensitive theological issues that have arisen over the centuries, such as the order of salvation, and it seems apposite to identify where Professor Gaffin's views fall on these matters.

Reformed debates concerning the proper relation between union with Christ, faith, and justification are hundreds of years old. In the seventeenth century, for example, the highly regarded New England divine, John Cotton—whose name and writings were quoted more often at the Westminster Assembly than John Calvin's—was at the center of these debates. The controversy was, like many intra-Reformed disputes, quite complex due to the Aristotelian-like categories used by theologians to explain causality in a full-orbed manner (e.g., principal, efficient, instrumental, material, formal, and final causes of salvation).

Regarding faith, a much-used distinction of the Reformed scholastic period concerned the difference between the act (*actus*) and the habit (*habitus*) of faith. The habit of faith gives the sinner the ability/potency that enables the act of faith to take place. The typical Reformed view is that actual faith justifies, but that habitual faith does not (*fides actualis justificat, non habitualis*). Cotton denied this premise, and by doing so he self-consciously held to views that were not typical of the mainstream of Reformed thought in his day. For Cotton, the habit of faith is the formal cause of justification, which precedes the act of faith. He was pressed on this view at a synod in New England, because his position that faith followed justification was not the typical Reformed view, but rather was associated with antinomianism. Almost all Reformed theologians held that faith precedes imputation. Faith enables the believer to be "mutually united" to Christ, resulting in what was sometimes called "ultimate union." Because of this, God imputes Christ's righteousness to the believing sinner. Both union and justification are contingent upon the act of faith. That is why Thomas Goodwin remarked that all of God's justifying acts depend on union with Christ. It also explains why, by and large, most Reformed theologians argued that faith was the antecedent condition for receiving justification. Thus, the imputation of Christ's righteousness to the believing sinner is mediate (i.e., through faith), not immediate (i.e., before faith). The role of faith in seventeenth-century Reformed dogmatics can hardly be overstated. Christ's works of impetration (i.e., salvation accomplished) are in a very real sense meaningless apart from his works of application. Against the antinomians, faith marks the transition of a sinner from being in a state of wrath to being in a state of grace. Faith is the means by which a sinner is brought into union with Christ. Any view that posits faith as a consequence of imputation (e.g., that of Cotton) is not the typical Reformed position. Readers will note that Professor Gaffin's view on the role of faith in the *ordo salutis* is unquestionably orthodox.

Therefore, what Melchior Leydekker said at the beginning of the eighteenth century, "Op de roeping, waar door het geloof en de vereeniging met Christus Jesus gegeven word / volgd de rechtveerdigmakinge" ("After calling, through which faith and union with Jesus Christ is given, follows justification"), could very well come from the pen of Professor Gaffin. Equally, Owen's contention that union with Christ is the cause of all other graces (e.g., justification, adoption, sanctification, and glorification) could also be affirmed by Professor Gaffin. In short, Reformed theologians have almost unanimously held that union with Christ is the ground of both justification and sanctification, and that Christ is the meritorious cause of both. But at the same time, union with Christ is not simply something that takes place only when faith is exercised. As our tradition has made perfectly clear, union with Christ is immanent, transient, and applicatory. In present-day Reformed parlance—which we also find articulated clearly in this book—we refer to these three stages as predestinarian, redemptive-historical, and mystical. The terms used in each era are different, but the concept remains the same. Each stage is contingent upon the previous stage, so that the ultimate goal of redemption planned and redemption accomplished is redemption applied.

Since the goal of redemption is union with the risen Lord, there seems little doubt that, if Paul has a center to his order of salvation, it is this doctrine. When other applied blessings, such as justification or sanctification, are made central, there are inevitably deleterious consequences for the Christian life, whereby incipient forms of antinomianism and legalism creep in. For example, a certain Lutheran view that justification precedes sanctification, so that it causes union with Christ and sanctification, ends up attributing to justification a renovative/transformative element. The notion that one applied benefit can cause another applied benefit has always perplexed me. But when union with Christ structures the whole of applied redemption, the aforementioned errors are dealt with better. This has to do with the fact that Christ's person, not simply his work or his applied benefits, must have the preeminence. Indeed, the gift of Christ's person is a greater gift to us than his benefits. As many of our finest divines have vigorously argued, there exists a priority of Christ's person over his work. Union with Christ helps us to keep this salient fact in mind. We are not simply recipients of his benefits; we also belong to him.

A second area of interest in present-day polemics regarding justification concerns the role of works at the final judgment. Balancing the doctrine of justification by faith alone with the teaching of Scripture that Christians will be judged "according to their works" remains a difficult task. Some imagine that the classical Reformed position on Romans 2:5–16 has in view only a hypothetical possibility, which in actual fact cannot be true of any sinner, whether redeemed or not. But many Reformed theologians did not adopt the hypothetical view of this disputed passage (though vv. 5–11 and 12–16 were sometimes distinguished), such as Martin Bucer, John Ball, Thomas Manton, Herman Witsius, Wilhelmus à Brakel, and Petrus van Mastricht. For example, Mastricht put forth the view that there are three stages of justification that should be "diligently observed." These are not different justifications, but distinct stages in the one justification by faith alone. In the first stage, "establishment," in which man is first justified, the efficacy and presence of works are entirely excluded for acquiring justification. In the second stage, "continuation," works have no efficacy, but works must be present, as we see in James 2:14–16. In the third stage, "consummation," in which believers gain possession of eternal life, good works have a certain "efficacy," insofar as God will not grant possession of eternal life unless they are present. Interestingly, Mastricht adduces Romans 2:7, 10 in support of his view. Like Mastricht, Professor Gaffin also rejects the view that Romans 2:5–16 is hypothetical. For that reason, both authors hold firmly to the Reformed view that good works are a necessary condition (consequent, not antecedent, to faith) for salvation. Spirit-wrought good works are not only *the way of life*, but also *the way to life/salvation* (see WLC 32). Yet the position expounded in this book is perhaps more persuasive than what one finds in Mastricht's significant work.

This last point allows me to address something else that will help readers to understand the worth of this book. The biblical-theological, redemptive-historical insights pioneered by Geerhardus Vos, Herman Ridderbos, and Richard Gaffin were anticipated in the early Reformed tradition. Some of our best early modern Reformed divines show an acute sensitivity to redemptive-historical concerns. The idea that Christ's resurrection and justification are also our resurrection and justification is not a recent invention. Indeed, Thomas Goodwin's remark that the matter (*materiale*) of justification is the obedience and death of Christ, but that the act of pronouncing us righteous (the *formale* of justification) depends on Christ's resurrection, which then ushers in the new creation, has strong affinities with the strongly redemptive-historical train of thought in this book.

With that in mind, Vos and the others were still pioneers in their field. But John Owen had already argued rather vigorously for the necessity of their approach. According to Owen, because of the way in which God has revealed himself in Scripture (i.e., not in the form of confessional documents), theologians need to be engaged in a process of ongoing exegetical reflection. In every age, there are different battles to be fought, which provide an opportunity for better restatements of the truth, as well as new insights into God's Word. Confessional theologians such as Owen did not merely rest on the truths discovered in the previous eras of ecclesiastical history, but hoped that Reformed theologians would continue the work they began. Indeed, this was due to the fact that error and heresy dress themselves up somewhat differently in each age. And discover new truths they did. The advancements by Vos, Ridderbos, and Gaffin concern the explicit integration and exposition of the role of eschatology in relation to soteriology, especially the recognition of the eschatological structure of the history of revelation culminating in the resurrection of Christ.

The reader of this book will quickly discover that Professor Gaffin deals with various current errors explicitly and implicitly. His irenic approach does not negate his ability to critique those with whom he disagrees. His explicit critique of the New Perspective(s) on Paul joins his implicit critique of a sort of antinomianism current in the church today, whereby the gospel (or salvation) is understood—practically, if not theoretically—almost exclusively in terms of justification. His arguments are devastating, not primarily because he confesses the truth as it has been expressed in our confessional history (which he does), but because his book is filled with rigorous exegesis of Scripture. Moreover, the eschatological focus (i.e., realized eschatology) of several core doctrines, particularly with reference to Christ's death and resurrection, enables Professor Gaffin to wed together nicely the redemptive-historical concerns, understood in terms of the *historia salutis*, and the applied soteriological realities, understood in terms of the *ordo salutis*. With these categories in place, the Christological focus of salvation accomplished and applied is maintained, union with Christ is given its proper significance, and the fullness of Paul's gospel is not reduced to forensic categories. For these reasons, the order of salvation must first be in Christ—he was called, justified, adopted, sanctified, and glorified—before it can be in his people. Moreover, Professor Gaffin carefully insists that justification has a logical and chronological priority to progressive sanctification—but the latter, not less than the former, still belongs to Paul's gospel! Thus, there is much in this book that is not original—and rightly so!—in terms of our Reformed theological heritage. But there is also much in this book that takes old truths and restates them with more clearly delineated categories in the wake of twentieth-century advancements in Pauline studies, as well as with fresh exegetical insights into key passages, such as 1 Corinthians 15:3–4.

With the above points in mind—and I could have made many more—allow me to express the reasons for my delight that this book will be made available again—this time, I hope, to a much wider audience. Here you have some of the most critical theological doctrines crystallized into a book that isn't hundreds of pages long. In this respect, Professor Gaffin is decidedly unlike the Puritans. Of course, each sentence is packed, and most readers will need to read this book a few times to understand his mind—and, I would say, more importantly, the mind of Paul. But your effort will be rewarded. You have the very best Reformed theology in front of you—Reformed theology that is neither Lutheran, nor antinomian, nor of the

New Perspective(s) on Paul. Instead, Professor Gaffin presents to us Reformed theology strengthened over time by clear theological categories and pain-staking exegesis of the Scriptures. I, for one, am glad that everything I have learned from my study of post-Reformation Reformed theologians has been vindicated by this penetrating and exegetically rigorous monograph on Paul and the order of salvation.

MARK JONES, VANCOUVER

Preface to the First Edition

THIS BOOK BEGAN as four lectures given for the annual School of Theology of Oak Hill Theological College, London, in May 2004, later expanded to five lectures given at the Seventh Annual Pastors Conference, sponsored by the session of the Auburn Avenue Presbyterian Church, Monroe, Louisiana, in January 2005. I take the opportunity here to express publicly my thanks for the warm hospitality I enjoyed on both occasions.

These lectures are presented here in four chapters, structured somewhat differently than when they were given, with a brief Epilogue added. Otherwise, I have kept to their scope and content, expanding for the most part only slightly at a number of places. This is in keeping with the purpose of the lectures, to highlight matters which, it seem to me, pastors and other teachers in the church and more generally interested students of the Bible need to be clear on and continue to think about as they concern themselves with Paul's theology. I hope my "academic peers" will find some value in what I have written, but they are not my primary audience.

Given this purpose, I have had to content myself at a number of places with having to assert rather than argue, with affirming instead of developing, at least in any extensive fashion. I am well aware that a much bigger book could be, and needs to be, written on the matters I have addressed. I ask the reader to keep in mind my primary concern with providing an overall perspective, without elaborating extensively, on a set of issues central in the teaching of Paul. That purpose accounts as well for what may strike some as the unevenness of the footnotes provided, which I have tried to keep to a minimum. The translations of biblical passages cited are my own, unless otherwise noted.

I deeply appreciate the invitation of Dr. David Peterson, Principal of Oak Hill College, to give these lectures and the attendant arrangement with Paternoster for their publication. The time spent with him and his colleagues, though brief, was one I continue to prize.

RICHARD B. GAFFIN JR.
WESTMINSTER THEOLOGICAL SEMINARY
MARCH 2006

Preface to the Second Edition

MY PLAN AT ONE POINT for a substantial expansion of the first edition has not materialized. With the continuing press of other commitments, I have had to forego doing that in order to avoid an even longer delay in republication.

The revisions in this edition are not extensive, though occasionally they are substantive. In a number of places I have rewritten to be as clear as I can, particularly in light of criticisms of the first edition. At several points I have addressed specific criticisms. A few footnotes have been added, as well as a Scripture index and an author/subject index.

My thanks to the publisher for undertaking this second edition, to Amanda Martin for her ready and efficient assistance, to James Scott for his careful reading of the manuscript and for proposing numerous improvements, to Dustyn Eudaly for his painstaking care in preparing the indices, and to Mark Jones for enhancing this volume with his Foreword.

RICHARD B. GAFFIN JR.
SEPTEMBER 2013

The Order of Salvation and the Theology of Paul

The Study of Paul Today

As many—perhaps most—readers will have at least some awareness, the study of Paul continues to be dominated by the so-called New Perspective on Paul, the substantial reassessment of Paul's theology that has emerged over the past several decades. Generalizations about this New Perspective need to be made with some caution. They are notoriously difficult, since the designation covers a spectrum of viewpoints that often diverge, sometimes even widely. Yet, if the label is at all meaningful, then some common concerns and convictions must be identifiable.[1]

Without attempting any kind of complete and documented description here, it seems fair to observe that what, as much as

---

1. The literature by this time is legion. For general surveys, see esp. G. Waters, *Justification and the New Perspectives on Paul: A Review and Response* (Phillipsburg, NJ: P&R, 2004), and S. Westerholm, *Perspectives Old and New on Paul: The "Lutheran" Paul and His Critics* (Grand Rapids: Eerdmans, 2004). Both these volumes, while on the whole fair in their depictions, are also substantially critical of the New Perspective. For a favorably disposed summary, see D. Garlington, *In Defense of the New Perspective on Paul: Essays and Reviews* (Eugene, OR: Wipf and Stock, 2005), 1–28 ("The New Perspective on Paul: Two Decades On"), and the personally orientated account of J. D. G. Dunn, *The New Perspective on Paul: Collected Essays* (Tübingen: Mohr Siebeck, 2005), 1–88 ("The New Perspective on Paul: Whence, What, Whither?").

I

anything, makes the New Perspective that, a new perspective, is a spectrum of reassessments of Paul decisively influenced by a reassessment of Second Temple Judaism in its various mainstream forms. In other words, the New Perspective on Paul is, more basically, a new perspective on Judaism in the Second Temple period; the reassessment of Paul stems from a basic reassessment of the Judaism of his time. It is worth noting here, moreover, that "new" here is relative. For the most part, this reassessment of Judaism, as applied to the study of Paul, is a matter of New Testament scholars arriving at conclusions about Second Temple Judaism and even about Paul that had already been reached by students of Judaism earlier in the twentieth century, notably by G. F. Moore and G. W. Montefiore. This primarily Protestant appropriation began approximately in the last quarter of the last century with the influential work of Krister Stendahl and E. P. Sanders, soon to be followed by others, notably James Dunn, who coined the expression "the New Perspective,"[2] and N. T. Wright.

A further fair generalization, particularly important for the concerns of this book, is the difference between the New Perspective, on the one hand, and the Reformation and subsequent confessional Protestantism, on the other, in their respective assessments of Pauline teaching—teaching that the Reformation tradition holds to be central for salvation. This difference especially relates to Paul's teaching on justification. New Perspective estimates of this difference vary, and its extent is a matter of ongoing debate. But a difference between the Reformation and New Perspective appraisals of Paul does exist. It is bound up with the New Perspective view that when Saul the Pharisee became Paul the Christian he did not, as the Reformation tradition holds, abandon a religion of personal salvation by works for one of salvation by grace through faith. Rather, he exchanged one understanding and experience of divine grace for another.

2. J. D. G. Dunn, "The New Perspective on Paul," *Bulletin of the John Rylands Library* 65 (1983): 95–122.

2

He repudiated a narrow, Jewish-centered view of God's electing grace for a broader, universal understanding, one that embraces not just Israel but all nations. One might say, on this view, that Paul, in becoming a Christian, went "from grace to grace."

Notably, the New Perspective sees Paul's teaching on justification by faith as reflecting concerns that are primarily (or even exclusively, for some of its proponents) corporate and ecclesiological, focused on the equal standing of Jewish and Gentile believers and how they are to relate to each other, rather than, as the Reformation holds, as critically constitutive for the salvation of individual sinners. In this way, the New Perspective decenters justification in Paul, not by questioning that it has an important place in his teaching, but by denying that it is central in his *soteriology*, especially as the Reformation tradition understands it to be central.

A basic consequence of these developments, particularly of this decentering of justification, as understood by the Reformation, is that the issue of the salvation of the individual has tended to become eclipsed or viewed as one about which Paul has relatively little concern or even interest. N. T. Wright, for instance, states that " 'the gospel' is not, for Paul, a message about 'how one gets saved,' in an individual and ahistorical sense." The gospel "is not, then, a system of how people get saved." The gospel, as Paul understands it, does not include what "in older theology would be called an *ordo salutis*, an order of salvation."[3] Justification is spoken of in a similar vein. "It cannot, that is, be made into an abstract or timeless system, a method of salvation randomly applied." Romans is "not . . . a detached statement of how people get saved, how they enter a relationship with God as individuals."[4]

3. N. T. Wright, *What Saint Paul Really Said* (Grand Rapids: Eerdmans, 1997), 40–41, 45, 60; cf. 32.
4. Ibid., 118, 131; cf. 129. I leave to the side here the question whether the pejorative use of "ahistorical," "timeless," "abstract," "detached," and "randomly

The New Perspective is preoccupied with broad, corporate, salvation-historical, covenantal, Israel-and-the-nations concerns. Properly so. Such concerns, as our own discussion will show, are undeniably not only present but prominent in Paul. But the New Perspective assesses them in a way that his teaching on matters related to individual salvation from sin is left aside as relatively unimportant and uncertain—or even dismissed as peripheral. If, for Paul, neither the gospel nor justification is directly concerned with the salvation of individuals, then it is at best unclear where Paul elsewhere addresses that concern and how he does it. Wright, for instance, says he is "perfectly comfortable with what people normally *mean* when they say 'the gospel.' I just don't think it is what Paul means."[5] Perhaps I have missed it, but it is not at all clear to me on what Pauline or other biblical basis he would support that normal meaning.

This state of affairs, as much as any other consideration, has prompted this book. In view of reservations and denials that have accompanied the emergence of the New Perspective and are resulting in a diminished interest in the question of the *ordo salutis* in Paul, it seems appropriate to test these reservations and denials by examining his theology, especially his soteriology, in terms of this question and the issues it raises. The controlling question I want to address throughout concerns Paul's understanding of how the individual receives salvation. Is that an appropriate or even meaningful question? If so, what place does Paul have for such reception? What does the application of salvation to sinners involve for him? Does he distinguish between salvation accomplished (*historia salutis*) and salvation

applied" in the statements quoted in this paragraph unfairly caricature the Reformation and evangelical tradition that is primarily within their purview. In my view, they do caricature, at least when the best and most important representatives of that tradition are considered.

5. Ibid., 41 (italics original).

4

applied (*ordo salutis*), and, if so, how important is the latter for him? What is the place of justification in his theology? Is it basic in his soteriology? These and related questions will occupy us.

While such questions are prompted by the development of the New Perspective on Paul, in addressing them here my primary concern is not to evaluate the New Perspective or interact in detail with particular views of its advocates. Rather, the New Perspective will remain in the background, coming into view only as it facilitates and to a certain extent situates my positive presentation of aspects of Paul's theology, primarily in his soteriology.

Regarding that positive presentation, it may be helpful to state at the outset that I see myself as working within the Reformation understanding of Paul and his soteriology, more particularly the understanding of Calvin and Reformed confessional orthodoxy, as I build on the biblical-theological work that has emerged within that tradition, particularly that of Herman Ridderbos and, before him, Geerhardus Vos, who have drawn attention to the controlling place of the redemptive-historical or covenant-historical dimension of his theology.[6]

Paul as Theologian—Some Foundations

Before we begin addressing the order or application of salvation in Paul, we will do well to spend some time on matters of a more general sort—matters that, it seems to me, pastors and other teachers in the church and, more broadly, other interested students of the Bible need to be clear about as they concern themselves with Paul's teaching, or "theology." While useful in its own right, this will serve to make explicit some of the controlling assumptions at work in this book as a whole. For the most part,

---

6. The major works of G. Vos and H. Ridderbos on Paul are, respectively, *The Pauline Eschatology* (1930; Grand Rapids: Baker, 1979), and *Paul: An Outline of His Theology* (trans. J. R. de Witt; Grand Rapids: Eerdmans, 1975).

I will have to assert and affirm, rather than argue or develop, at least in any full fashion.

Biblical Theology and Redemptive-Historical Interpretation

Paul's teaching, especially any of its major themes, involves so-called biblical theology. Since there are widely differing, even contradictory, views of what such a biblical-theological enterprise entails, I should make my own understanding clear. Doing so will also reveal some of my basic commitments on matters of method.[7]

Biblical theology gives attention to the distinctive contribution of each of the biblical writers within his immediate historical circumstances or situatedness. That involves taking into account the fully "occasional" character of their writings, that is, the concrete concerns and specific problems of the original addressees. For reasons we will note presently, such an approach is especially called for in the case of Paul.

A biblical-theological approach, however, must recognize that each writer is part of a much larger scenario, a much larger *historical* scenario. Each with his distinctive contribution functions in the unfolding history of God's self-revelation. God's verbal self-revelation has its rationale as it is tethered to, and is a part within, the larger flow of the overall history of redemption. It functions as accompanying revelatory word, we may fairly generalize, to attest and interpret redemptive deed. In view here, globally considered, is the history that begins with the entrance of human sin into the original creation, which God saw was "very good" (Gen. 1:31), and then moves forward, largely incorporating along the way the history of Israel, God's chosen

---

7. My comments in the rest of this section follow esp. along the lines of the classic, still important treatment of G. Vos, *Biblical Theology: Old and New Testaments* (Grand Rapids: Eerdmans, 1948), Preface, 11–27 ("Introduction: The Nature and Method of Biblical Theology").

covenant people, until it reaches its culmination, its omega point, in the person and saving work of Jesus Christ, God's final and supreme self-revelation.

The generalizations made in the preceding paragraph are in need of two important qualifications. First, particularly with an eye to special, or verbal, revelation, the terms "covenant history" and "covenant-historical" are more accurate than "redemptive history" and "redemptive-historical." While special revelation for the most part is redemptive, coming after the fall, pre-fall, preredemptive special revelation should not be overlooked or denied as an *integral* aspect of the covenantal communion, the bond of fellowship, that existed between God and his image-bearing creatures before the fall. Natural, or general, revelation (including "natural law") was never meant to function independently, apart from special revelation, whether before or after the fall.[8]

Second, it is fair to say, as a generalization, that verbal revelation is invariably focused on God's activity in history as Creator and Redeemer. It should not be missed, however, that with that historical focus verbal revelation at points refers beyond God's activity in history to his aseity, his self-existence, to his absolute freedom and independence from creation and history. This is beautifully intimated, for instance, in Isaiah 57:15, "For thus says the One who is high and lifted up, who inhabits eternity, whose name is Holy: 'I dwell in the high and holy place, and also with him who is of a contrite and lowly spirit, to revive the spirit of the lowly, and to revive the heart of the contrite'" (ESV).

The clearest, most explicit biblical warrant for the fundamental redemptive-historical, history-of-revelation construct in view here is the overarching assertion with which Hebrews begins: "God, having spoken in the past to the fathers through the prophets at many times and in various ways, has in these last days spoken to us in his Son" (1:1–2a). This opening statement, umbrella-like, covers the message of Hebrews in its entirety. As

8. On preredemptive special revelation, see esp. Vos, *Biblical Theology*, 31–32.

such, it is fairly seen, even more broadly, as providing an overall outlook on the history of redemption and revelation as a whole.

This declaration captures three interrelated aspects of God's "speech," which, I take it, includes deed-revelation as well as word-revelation (that is, verbal revelation in the strict sense). (1) Revelation is expressly in view as a historical process. (2) The diversity involved in this process is accented, particularly for old covenant revelation, revelation through the prophets, by the two adverbs translated "at many times and in various ways," which for emphasis are placed at the beginning of the construction in the original Greek. This diversity, whether or not it is within the author's immediate purview, entails giving commensurate attention to the diverse modes and various literary genres that mark the history of revelation. (3) Christ is the "last days" endpoint of this history, which is nothing less than the eschatological goal of the entire redemptive-revelatory process.[9]

These three points bring us to an all-important observation about the study of Paul. We may say with Geerhardus Vos that Paul is "the greatest constructive mind ever at work on the data of Christianity." Or, as Albert Schweitzer, from a quite contrary perspective, has evocatively put it, Paul is "the patron saint of thought in Christianity."[10] Nonetheless, Paul's theological genius, though unquestionably profound, is not our ultimate interest in considering his teaching. Nor is that interest finally his religious experience, though from every indication it was deep and exemplary. Rather, our deepest concern with him is as he is an apostle—that is, as he is an instrument of God's revelation, authorized by the exalted Christ to attest and interpret the salvation manifested in Christ. Our abiding preoccupation is the

9. For more extensive discussion of redemptive-historical interpretation, see my chapters in S. E. Porter and B. M. Stovell, eds., *Biblical Hermeneutics: Five Views* (Downers Grove, IL: IVP Academic, 2012), 89–110, 174–87.

10. Vos, *Pauline Eschatology*, 149; A. Schweitzer, *The Mysticism of Paul the Apostle* (trans. W. Montgomery; New York: H. Holt, 1931), 377.

revelatory word that comes through Paul, focused on Christ's climactic, redemptive deed.

As we deal with Paul's teaching, then, we should want it to be said of ourselves, above all, what he himself said in 1 Thessalonians 2:13 about the Thessalonian church's response to his preaching, namely that they "accepted it not as the word of men"—though it was manifestly his and bore all the marks of his personality as someone living within the first-century Mediterranean world and having his roots in Second Temple Judaism—"but as what it truly is, the word of God." Ultimately and properly considered, Paul's teaching is God's word. This, I take it, is not just a pious but largely irrelevant patina on our work that may be safely stripped away and effectively ignored as we go about interpreting him. Rather, at stake here is a matter of sober, scientific, methodological, academic necessity for studying Paul—what, as he himself says, is "truly" (*alēthōs*) the case.

That Paul's teaching is God's word is true formally as well as materially—true not just in its content, but also in its oral and written *form*. To deny that the text is God's word, or to allege some factor of discontinuity between the text and God's word, or to find a tension between the text as a linguistic phenomenon, of purely human origin and so questionable and fallible, and a message with an allegedly divine referent dialectically embedded in that text, is to construe Paul in a modern or postmodern way that he would simply find foreign. At least that is so if we are to take 2 Timothy 3:16 and similar passages at face value.[11]

11. The passive verbal adjective *theopneustos*, "God-breathed" (2 Tim. 3:16), predicates of the documents that constitute "Scripture" a permanent, enduring quality resulting from their origin, and is best understood as pointing to God as their primary and ultimate author. This conclusion has been firmly established in the works of B. B. Warfield, not to mention others. Efforts made to evade it, such as that made recently by C. D. Allert (*A High View of Scripture?* [Grand Rapids: Baker Academic, 2007], 153–56), who cites and attempts to refute Warfield, remain quite unsuccessful; see especially Warfield's *The Inspiration and Authority of the Bible* (Phillipsburg, NJ: Presbyterian

A couple of implications of the word-of-God character of Paul's teaching may be noted here. One important methodological consideration is that, with all due attention being given to his immediate historical context, including relevant extracanonical texts and materials, in interpreting his letters the context that is not only *primary* but *privileged* is the *canonical* context. For any given passage in Paul, the ultimately controlling context is the expanding horizon of contexts provided by the rest of Scripture, beginning with his letters as a whole. This basic hermeneutical stance, it bears stressing, is not bound up with some abstract Scripture principle, as it is wont to be dismissed by some, but is anchored in a consideration already noted, the *redemptive-historical* factor. Paul's letters have their origin, their integral place, and their intended function within the organically unfolding history of revelation, and Scripture as a whole, the canon, with its own production being a part of that history, provides our only normative access to it.

A key part of Paul's theology as God's word is its *essential clarity*. As the Reformation was granted to recognize and confess regarding Scripture as a whole, the assumption, indeed the conviction, throughout this book is that for the church Paul's teaching in its central elements is clear. Just what some of those "central elements" are will occupy us later.

The primary sources for understanding and elaborating Paul's theology I take to be all thirteen of his New Testament letters and also pertinent materials from the latter half of Acts, in particular his speeches and other discourse material recorded there.

The Problem of Interpreting Paul

The essential clarity of Paul's theology must not be affirmed at the expense of ignoring a problem. A couple of rather arrest-

and Reformed, 1948), 245–296 ("The God-Inspired Scripture"), as well as other pertinent chapters in that volume.

ing quotes point up the problem. Albert Schweitzer recounts a remark of Franz Overbeck to Adolf von Harnack, made one day when these two late-nineteenth-century New Testament scholars were together: "No one has ever understood Paul and the only one who did understand him, Marcion, misunderstood him."[12] More recently, Herman Ridderbos has surmised that in Paul's account of his ministry in 2 Corinthians 11:23–26, we have an apt description of the history of the interpretation of Paul: "beaten times without number, often in danger of death . . . shipwrecked three times . . . in danger from my nation, in danger from the Gentiles . . . in danger among false brothers"![13]

The issue here is not to what extent these and similar statements are warranted. Certainly Overbeck's paradoxically expressed pessimism is not. But such assessments do point up an undeniable state of affairs: the problematic nature of Pauline interpretation down through the history of the church to the present. In fact, the New Testament itself anticipates this state of affairs. This not only points up the antiquity of the problem of interpreting Paul, but also and more importantly puts it in an explicitly canonical perspective.

The reference, of course, is to the generalization made about Paul's letters in 2 Peter 3:16: "In all his [Paul's] letters" (whatever may have been the specific contents of the Pauline corpus circulating at that time) there are "some things that are difficult to understand." These things, Peter goes on to add, bringing out the dark side of the picture as a permanent warning to the church, "the ignorant and unstable twist, as they do the other Scriptures, to their own destruction." Notice, by the way, pertinent to our earlier point about Paul's theology being God's word, that this statement is New Testament evidence that already at the time

---

12. Schweitzer, *Mysticism*, 39 n. 1.

13. H. Ridderbos, "Terugblik en uitzicht," in *De dertiende apostel en het elfde gebod: Paulus in de loop der eeuwen*, ed. G. C. Berkouwer and H. A. Oberman (Kampen: Kok, 1971), 190.

2 Peter was written, Paul's letters as a whole were put on a par with the Old Testament and viewed as Scripture.

Peter's assertion of the overall difficulty in understanding Paul's letters prompts us to ask what constitutes that difficulty. Immediately come to mind all the limitations there are on the side of the interpreter, including the ignorance, sometimes sinful, and the sinful perversity we bring to the text in varying degrees. But Peter seems to have in view something distinct from the culpable distortion he mentions, an *inherent* difficulty, a difficulty intrinsic to the text. When we ask about that difficulty, no doubt more than one factor is involved.

For instance, according to 1 Corinthians 2:10, in a context where Paul brings into view considerations basic to his ministry as a whole, he says that the revelation granted to him through the Spirit involves "the deep things of God." The central clarity of Paul's teaching flows out of, as it has its roots in, the impenetrable depths of God's incomprehensibility. For example, the doxology at the end of Romans 11, arresting as it is edifying, is an expression of that incomprehensibility.

To be noted here as well for subsequent generations of the church, like ours, is the difficulty bound up with what at first glance is a much more prosaic factor, the "occasional" nature of his writings already noted. Paul does not provide us with doctrinal treatises, but with letters—genuine letters directed to concrete conditions and problems in specific church situations. A notably pastoral, "practical" concern is always present, even in those sections of Romans where doctrinal reflection is most apparent. On balance, we may say, Paul's letters present, even in their occasional and often doxological character, a unified structure of thought, a coherence of theological thinking.

So a real difficulty in interpreting Paul is that in his writings we encounter a thinker of undeniably reflective and constructive genius with a decidedly doctrinal bent, but only as he directs himself to specific church situations and problems and in doing so expresses himself in a way that is largely non-formalized theologically, in a nonsystematic or nontopical format. Paul is a theologian who is accessible only through his letters and records of his sermons. Although his letters are not theological treatises, in them we undeniably encounter Paul the theologian.

Another factor compounding the difficulty, especially for us at the historical distance we are, is that some of his letters are written largely against the background of a good deal of previous personal contact and extensive instruction now unknown to us in detail. A good example of this is his teaching on "the man of sin" in 2 Thessalonians 2:1–12, where in verse 6 he writes, "Now you know." What Paul seems to assume as more or less self-evident to his original readers has left subsequent generations of interpreters down to the present thoroughly perplexed and unable to arrive at any real consensus, a state of affairs that prompts from Vos, toward the end of his own lengthy treatment of the passage, the wry comment to the effect that we will have to wait on its fulfillment for its best and definitive exegesis![14]

An analogy I have found useful over the years is to compare Paul's letters to the visible portion of an iceberg. What projects above the surface is but a small fraction of the total mass, which remains largely submerged, so that what is taken in, particularly at a first glance, may prove deceptive. This point is made less pictorially by the hermeneutical principle expressed in chapter 1, section 6 of the Westminster Confession of Faith, that the teaching of Scripture is not only its express statements but also what follows "by good and necessary consequence." Particularly in the case of Paul, we are going to make full sense of his letters as a whole, of his theology, only as we are prepared to wrestle with matters of "good and necessary consequence" and with

14. Vos, *Pauline Eschatology*, 133.

the sometimes nettlesome questions that emerge. This state of affairs in large part makes the extensive interpretation of Paul the arduous, even precarious, enterprise to which 2 Peter 3:16 alerts us.

With this factor of difficulty highlighted, an important caveat needs to be made. We must not stress difficulty to the point of losing sight of the more basic clarity to be recognized and affirmed. After all, Peter did not say that "all things" in Paul are "difficult to understand," but only "some things."

Paul as a Theologian

All along I have been speaking of Paul's "theology" and referring to him as a "theologian." For many, that will not be a problem, but this way of speaking warrants some clarification, since for some it is questionable at best. The perceived danger here is that we will, as it could be put, "drag Paul down to our level." Viewing Paul as a theologian suggests that he and his theology have at the most only relative authority, that however else we might want to privilege him, his theology has no more authority in principle than any other. This worry is by no means an imaginary one. That is clear from historical-critical approaches to Paul over the past century and a half, particularly as one surveys major works on his theology from F. C. Baur (1845) to James Dunn (1998).[15]

What offsets this leveling danger is appreciating Paul's identity as an apostle, at least if we understand apostleship properly. In accordance with our earlier comments on his teaching being God's word, we must not lose sight of the formal authoritative significance of his apostolic identity. Careful exegesis, which I omit here, will show that an apostle of Christ is someone uniquely authorized by the exalted Christ to speak authorita-

15. Baur appears to have the distinction of being the first to publish a theology of Paul.

tively for him. Regarding this authority, the apostle is as Christ himself.[16]

Paul the theologian, then, is Paul the apostle. That points to the God-breathed origin and authority of his teaching, its character as the word of God. It highlights the radical, categorical difference there is between his theology and post-apostolic theology. His teaching, along with the teaching of the other biblical writers, is Spirit-borne, canonical, and foundational. All subsequent theology, including ours, ought to be Spirit-*led* (Rom. 8:14), but, unlike Paul's, it is not Spirit-*borne* (2 Peter 1:21). Ours is noncanonical, no more than derivative of his.

But with that said, the appropriateness and value of approaching Paul as a theologian should not be missed. Again, that value resides in the redemptive-historical factor already noted. With the exception of the situation before the fall, about which we know relatively little since the biblical record concerning it is sparse, all verbal revelation, including Paul's teaching, is a function of the history of redemption and situated at some point in that history. In the case of Paul, like that of the other New Testament writers, redemptive history has reached its climactic endpoint in the death and resurrection of Christ and awaits his return.

Along with the important differences between Paul's theology and ours, there is much that we have in common. In terms of the history of redemption, we share with him and the other New Testament writers a common redemptive-historical *focus* and, further, we do so within a common redemptive-historical *context*. In this regard, 1 Thessalonians 1:9–10 is particularly instructive. There Paul speaks of how that church "turned to God from idols to serve the living and true God and to wait for

16. Out of the vast body of literature on apostolicity in the NT, including apostolic authority, see esp. H. Ridderbos, *Redemptive History and the New Testament Scriptures* (trans. H. De Jongste; rev. R. B. Gaffin, Jr.; Phillipsburg, NJ: Presbyterian and Reformed, 1988), 1–52.

his Son from heaven, whom he raised from the dead, Jesus, who rescues us from the wrath to come."

Here is a perennial word to the church, good for all times and places until Jesus comes again, one that captures as well as any the basic identity of the church. Christians are those who have renounced, however imperfectly, every idolatry for the service of the living and true God, a service that is bracketed and fundamentally conditioned by Christ's death and resurrection and his return. So our theologizing, too, including our treatment of Paul's theology, ought to be seen as just one aspect of this redemptive-historically conditioned "waiting service." This, I take it, is one factor that protects our theology from undue abstractions and promotes its true concreteness. This, if you will, is its ultimate "contextualization."

At issue here, in viewing Paul as a theologian, is whether Scripture, as canon, not only provides the content of our theology, but also contributes to our theological method—how we do theology. If our concern is to uphold "the system of doctrine" "taught" or "contained" in the Bible,[17] then especially in our systematic theology we ought to be alert to the ways in which that systematizing and integrating task is in evidence in the New Testament itself and begins to surface there.

In underlining this approach to our theological task, I do not understand myself to be saying anything other than what is affirmed in the Westminster Confession of Faith, 1.6, namely that the teaching of Scripture is not only what is "expressly set down in Scripture," but also what "by good and necessary consequence may be deduced from Scripture." However, if there is a plus involved in what we are saying here, it is that recognizing continuity, particularly redemptive-historical continuity, between ourselves and the New Testament writers, especially Paul, not only in the content but also in the

17. The reference is to the formula for subscription to the Westminster Standards used in a number of denominations and institutions.

method of our theology, may contribute to ensuring that "the good and necessary consequence . . . deduced" is truly good and necessary.

Biblical Theology and Systematic Theology

Viewing Paul as a theologian in the way we have viewed him prompts a couple of observations on the much-mooted issue of the relationship between biblical theology and systematic theology. First, in exploring Paul's theology as an aspect of doing biblical theology, we should be aware that we are involved as well in doing systematic theology, or better, that our biblical-theological explorations will inevitably have systematic-theological repercussions. This is so because systematic theology ought to be radically nonspeculative in the sense that its very existence depends upon sound biblical interpretation. Exegesis is its lifeblood, so that the method of systematic theology is fundamentally exegetical.

Accordingly, systematic theology may be aptly characterized as large-scale plot analysis, that is, the presentation under various topics (*loci*), appropriate to the biblical metanarrative (God, creation, man, sin, salvation, the church, etc.), of the *unified* teaching of the Bible as a *whole*. Its distinguishing concern is to bring out and highlight the harmony, the concordant unity, that there is in the biblical documents in their historical variety and diversity. That God himself is the primary author of these documents guarantees that, despite remaining questions and uncertainties that we will always have, Scripture does have such harmony.

Biblical theology, then, is indispensable for providing and regulating the exegesis on which systematic theology is staked and from which it derives. So it is quite wrongheaded to view biblical theology, as do many (primarily those with a historical-critical orientation), as a purely historical-descriptive task, and systematic theology as a contemporary-normative statement of Christian truth, with each discipline going its separate way, more or less independently. The result is a dichotomization or even polarization between them that continues to be widespread at present. No less polarizing in its effect and bound to lead to hopelessly confused results is the similar approach that sees biblical theology as concerned more or less exclusively with the "humanity," or human side, of the Bible, with its historically rooted origin and contents, while leaving requisite concern with the divine side to systematic theology.

Instead, there should be a back-and-forth, reciprocal relationship between the two in their common concern with Scripture as God-breathed and normative. Specifically, to be involved with Pauline theology is to be engaged at least implicitly in systematic theology, within a common redemptive-historical context and with the same redemptive-historical focus. This is particularly unavoidable in the case of Paul. The closely intertwined histories of theology and Pauline interpretation, especially since the Reformation, make that reciprocity clear enough. For this reason, it will be appropriate at points throughout this volume to orient our treatment of Paul and relate our findings to developments in the history of theology.

Second, keeping in mind what has already been said above about the canonical context as privileged in interpreting Paul, it is essential for the biblical-theological task, and so for systematic theology, that Paul's theology not be studied in isolation or as an end in itself. It needs always to be developed, reciprocally, along with and in the light of other New Testament, as well as Old Testament, teaching. This canonical control is, it seems to me, a consideration not sufficiently appreciated, typically by approaches associated with the New Perspective on Paul. One can become so absorbed with Paul's theology on its own terms and in its own immediate historical context, that it becomes unduly detached from its canonical context and its divinely intended function within Scripture as a whole.

In this regard, the negative example of Marcion, already in the second century, serves as a permanent warning to the church against a one-sided "Paulinism." A tendentious appeal to Paul in support of a distortion of the gospel is by no means an imaginary danger. Not without reason, Tertullian was reportedly prompted to call Paul *hereticorum apostolos*, "the apostle of heretics." And subsequent instances of misguided appeals to Paul throughout church history bear out the aptness of this description.

With these general reflections on the study of Paul in mind, we may now begin to consider his teaching on the order of salvation—on the individual Christian's appropriation of salvation.

The Order of Salvation and the "Center" of Paul's Theology

THE EXPRESSION *ORDO SALUTIS* in its conventional usage has in view the logical and/or causal, or even at points chronological, "order" or sequence of various discrete saving acts and benefits, as these are applied and occur within the actual life of the individual sinner.[1] This usage clearly presupposes a more basic distinction, the distinction between salvation accomplished and salvation applied. Salvation in its ongoing application, which this ordering is concerned to explicate, is to be distinguished categorically from salvation in its once-for-all accomplishment. With an eye to the redemptive-historical character of that completed accomplishment, and following Herman Ridderbos in coining a Latin counterpart, the distinction between the application and the accomplishment of salvation may be expressed by distinguishing generically between *ordo salutis* (the order of salvation) and *historia salutis* (the history of salvation).[2]

1. Assuming the secondary sources are correct, the term *ordo salutis* in this sense was first used in the eighteenth century within emerging Pietism, from where it was taken over and eventually became widely used in both Lutheran and Reformed orthodoxy. Standard in Reformed theology is this order: calling, regeneration, faith and repentance, justification, adoption, sanctification (including perseverance), and glorification.

2. This distinction (*historia salutis–ordo salutis*) appears to have originated with Herman Ridderbos. I have not seen it earlier than in his essay "The

In raising the question of an *ordo salutis* in Paul at this point, I have in view the more general sense just indicated, a concern with the application of salvation as distinct from its once-for-all accomplishment, *historia salutis*.[3] Does Paul have an *ordo salutis*? That is, is he in fact concerned with salvation in its ongoing application? Does he, along with his undeniably redemptive-historical (*historia salutis*) orientation, give attention to matters of the individual appropriation of salvation? If so, is a particular order in the application of salvation present in his teaching? Does such a pattern and matters related to it lie within the scope of his interests?

Or, alternatively, does he have little interest in such matters—little concern, as we noted in the previous chapter that some are currently saying, with "how one gets saved"?[4] Put another way, is Luther's agonized question about obtaining salvation from a gracious God totally foreign to Paul or at least one in which he would not be particularly interested?

The question of the order of salvation in Paul is to be answered in the affirmative. That can be seen initially, in a provisional, prima facie fashion, in the differentiating and conditional way in which Paul speaks of faith. The church in Thessalonica, for instance, is exhorted to pray that "the word of the Lord" will spread with success, among other reasons, "for not all have faith" (2 Thess. 3:1–2). In the face of death, Christians, as those who "believe," are not like "the rest who do not have hope" (1 Thess. 4:13–14). Also, with Christ explicitly as the focus of faith, "if you . . . believe . . . you will be saved" (Rom. 10:9). Similarly, the ques-

---

Redemptive-Historical Character of Paul's Preaching," in *When the Time Had Fully Come: Studies in New Testament Theology* (Grand Rapids: Eerdmans, 1957), 44–60, at 48, 49. It occurs repeatedly in his *Paul: An Outline of His Theology* (trans. J. R. de Witt; Grand Rapids: Eerdmans, 1975), e.g., 14, 45, 63, 91.

3. The specific elements in Paul's "order" and how they are related to each other will appear as our discussion unfolds.

4. N. T. Wright, *What Saint Paul Really Said* (Grand Rapids: Eerdmans, 1997), 60.

tion of the Philippian jailor ("What must I do to be saved?")—an explicitly *ordo salutis* inquiry—is met with the answer, "Believe . . . and you will be saved" (Acts 16:31).

So the salvation accomplished by Christ is realized, or effectually appropriated, only where faith, focused on him, is present. In this regard, everything turns on faith, and all that is effected "by faith." Thoroughly Pauline, then, is the principle of seventeenth-century orthodox Protestant dogmatics: "Without application, redemption is not redemption."[5]

This reference to faith prompts a brief comment on the title of this book. Many readers will recognize that it echoes 2 Corinthians 5:7, "We walk [live] by faith, not by sight." Within the immediate context, Paul's primary concern is with the bodily resurrection of Christians, as well as their being with Christ apart from the body at death. Verse 7, then, points up that the resurrection of the body is a future hope, not a present, perceptible reality.

But without losing its specific focus on bodily resurrection, this statement with its aphoristic ring fairly serves as a basic window on the whole of what Paul, with an eye on the future, has to say about the church's present possession of the salvation revealed in Christ and about the Christian life. As I hope will become clear as we proceed, it provides a valuable lens for looking at key aspects of that teaching.

The "Center" of Paul's Theology

If our overall concern is the question of an *ordo salutis* in Paul, or how he views the actual appropriation of salvation in its individual and corporate aspects, then an issue of method or procedure faces us. How should we go about answering this

---

5. "Dempta applicatione, redemptio non est redemptio," cited by H. Bavinck in the course of a lengthy and important treatment of the *ordo salutis* ("De Heilsorde") in *Gereformeerde Dogmatiek* (Kampen: Kok, 1976), 3:520; cf. H. Bavinck, *Reformed Dogmatics* (trans. J. Vriend; Grand Rapids: Baker, 2006), 3:523–24.

question as Paul would? How can we address it in a way that minimizes the risk of imposing an agenda of concerns that is foreign to his outlook or otherwise distorts it?

This procedural concern is alleviated, it seems to me, by relating our inquiry as a whole to the center of Paul's theology and coming at it in terms of that center. Some today, however, have a problem with talking about Paul's theology having a center. So we need, at least briefly, to address that question here. Does Paul's theology have a "center"?

Despite the reservations of some, it seems difficult to deny that he does, particularly if that notion is not maintained rigidly or too narrowly, as if there were a single key concept, like election or salvation or even God, from which everything can be shown to be deduced. That is not the case. There is no such *Zentraldogma* in Paul. At the same time, however, neither does the ad hoc, occasional character of his letters provide us with a proverbial wax nose, so that we can make of them virtually whatever we will.

By the metaphor of a "center," I mean that in Paul's letters an overall set of concerns is identifiable, in which some matters are plainly more important for him than others. Certainly, Paul may be approached from a variety of perspectives, and it is valuable to do so, but each of his various concerns is not equally important or controlling. Recognizing this points to a circle of interests, in which each is more or less central, with room for debate in some instances as to relative centrality. Assuming, then, that in this sense Paul's theology has a center, what is it? What is the locus of his centering concerns, and, more importantly, how do we go about identifying it properly?

There is perhaps more than one way to answer this question. However, it seems that we do so best, most safely and usefully, if we proceed by identifying those passages in Paul that more or less clearly have a summarizing or synoptic function, whether in his words or where he may be utilizing an already existing formulation. Our interest, in other words, is in statements that express more or less unmistakably his core concerns.

Without trying here to provide a complete survey of such materials, there is, to begin with, the elemental confession, "Jesus is Lord" (1 Cor. 12:3), and, expanded, the similar faith-confession of Jesus as resurrected Lord in Romans 10:9–10. A passage in which Paul highlights factors basic to his apostolic ministry as a whole, including what may fairly be seen as his theological epistemology, is 1 Corinthians 1:18–3:22. In 2:2 he asserts, "For I resolved to know nothing while I was with you, except Jesus Christ and him crucified." Paul's exclusive and comprehensive epistemic commitment is to the crucified Christ. In a similar vein is Galatians 6:14, "May I never boast, except in the cross of our Lord Jesus Christ." Pertinent as well is 2 Timothy 2:8, perhaps adapting an existing creedal summary, "Remember Jesus Christ, raised from the dead . . . according to my gospel" (NIV: "this is my gospel").

In the opening chapter of Romans, as Paul is "set apart for the gospel of God" (v. 1), that gospel, he says, again perhaps using a preexisting formulation, concerns "his Son, who was born of the seed of David according to the flesh and declared to be Son of God in power according to the Spirit of holiness by the resurrection from the dead" (vv. 3–4). Romans 4:25, perhaps another pre-Pauline confessional fragment, is certainly intended as a summary encapsulation: "He was delivered up for our sins and was raised for our justification."

What is plain enough is the profile emerging from such summary statements. Others that might be proposed, like Philippians 2:6–11, will not change it. The focus is on Christ—not in an undefined or indefinite way, but specifically in his death and/or resurrection.

What is worth recalling at this point, because it is particularly applicable to Paul, is the observation made at least as early as Calvin that in Scripture references to the death alone or to the resurrection alone are synecdochic.[6] That is, to speak of the one in its significance always has in view the other in its significance. They are unintelligible apart from each other; each conditions the meaning of the other.

1 Corinthians 15:3–4

The statements just noted have been cited with an eye toward identifying the center of Paul's theology. To that end, what would seem particularly useful are statements that are sufficiently nuclear yet have enough detail to identify an appropriate and adequately inclusive circumference of issues and concerns. In this regard, a passage that commends itself as perhaps most helpful and forthcoming, at least more so than most other proposals, is 1 Corinthians 15:3–4. There Paul perhaps, though not certainly, utilizes an already existing confessional fragment:

> For I passed on to you as of first importance, what I also received: that Christ died for our sins according to the Scriptures, that he was buried, that he was raised on the third day according to the Scriptures.

Within the overall context of Paul's teaching, this statement prompts several initial observations, which I will note briefly and then elaborate. First, in the prepositional phrase, literally "among first things" (*en prōtois*), "first," as virtually all commentators take it, almost certainly has a qualitative, not a temporal sense; most English translations properly render it "of first importance." So, Paul is explicit, his paramount concerns have their focus, their center, in Christ's death and resurrection.

Further, in view of verses 1–2 ("Now I remind you, brothers, of the gospel I preached to you"), this center is plainly the

6. J. Calvin, *Institutes of the Christian Religion* (trans. F. L. Battles; ed. J. T. McNeill; Library of Christian Classics; 2 vols.; Philadelphia: Westminster, 1960), 1:521 (2.16.13).

center of his gospel. That, in turn, prompts an even broader observation. At verse 1, Paul is best read as reflecting on his ministry as a whole among the Corinthians. In view is not just a part of his proclamation, not just an aspect of his teaching, but his message in its entirety. That disposes us to say globally that Paul's theology is his gospel; his is a "gospel-theology." Or, viewed in terms of expanding concentric circles, the center of Paul's theology is the gospel, and at the center of that gospel are the death and resurrection of Christ. The focus of the whole, its gospel-center, is Christ's death and resurrection.

Second, his death and resurrection are not in view as bare, isolated, uninterpreted facts. Two things are stipulated. Their occurrence is "according to the Scriptures." That is, they have their meaning as they fulfill the Jewish scriptures, as they involve fulfillment of the Old Testament. Further, the death is said to be "for our sins." At the center of Paul's gospel-theology, then, Christ's death, together with his resurrection, as the fulfillment of Scripture, has its significance in relation to human ("our") sin and its consequences.

This brings us to a baseline conclusion following from this passage and reinforced by others already noted: at the center of Paul's theology are Christ's death and resurrection, or, expressed more broadly, his messianic suffering and glory, his humiliation and exaltation.

With this conclusion and with an eye toward the issue of the order or application of salvation in Paul, it needs to be appreciated that the center of Paul's gospel-theology, its primary focus, is not one or other applied benefit of Christ's work—say, justification by faith or the work of the Spirit in believers—but that work itself, culminating in his exaltation. In other words, as we raise the question of the *ordo salutis* in Paul, we need to keep in mind that his controlling focus is the *historia salutis*, not the *ordo salutis*. Or, to avoid leaving the impression of a false disjunction at this point, we should say that he is certainly concerned with matters of individual appropriation, but only as those concerns are integrally tethered to, and flow from, his redemptive-historical focus.

Does this conclusion "decenter" justification, as some allege, or the work of the Spirit in Paul's teaching? Not at all. I hope to make that clear as we proceed. But it is a conclusion that puts such benefits in proper perspective. This basic perspective does represent something of a difference in accent from what has largely been true since the Reformation. Here, in bold strokes, we may note the developments that have produced this shift.

The widespread perception is that for the Reformation, in its conflict with Rome, the center of Paul's theology, as much as anything, was justification. But putting it like that is, strictly speaking, anachronistic. The Reformers and early post-Reformation theologians did not think in terms of Paul's theology; that is, his teaching was not treated as a distinct unit. The biblical-theological idea of "Paul's theology" arose with the historical-critical method that emerged from the Enlightenment. As noted earlier, F. C. Baur (1845) appears to have been the first to write a theology of Paul.

However, as a generalization, it is surely fair to say that in the Reformation tradition Paul is read primarily as the preacher or exponent of justification *sola fide*. In other words, legal or forensic concerns—concerns related to sin as guilt and to release from the guilt incurred by sin and the attendant wrath of God—are found to be central. These judicial concerns have been held to be controlling for him.

Virtually from the beginning, however, some have challenged this Reformation perception by maintaining that justification is not that prominent a concern for Paul. In view here, for the most part, are later developments in the historical-critical mainstream. Some (e.g., Albert Schweitzer) have even argued that justification is a subsidiary matter, no more than a tactical teaching, utilized under some circumstances but not others. Instead, on this view, Paul's primary interest is related to sin as a disrupting and destructive power and so has to do with personal communion with Christ and the work of the Holy Spirit involving inner renewal and personal change. Matters variously dubbed "ethical," "spiritual," "mystical," "relational," or "participatory" are held to be central.

All in all, from the Reformation until relatively recently, the debate about the center of Paul's theology has tended to focus on the personal appropriation of salvation—on concerns about its application, or, in other words, on matters related to the *ordo salutis*. More specifically, the question at issue has been whether that center is the individual's justification by faith or the inward work of the Holy Spirit in personal renewal and sanctification, and how justification and sanctification relate to each other.

Increasingly over the course of the last century, to fill out this brief historical sketch, a new consensus concerning Paul emerged across a broad front in biblical studies. This happened in tandem with a reassessment of the kingdom proclamation of Jesus. It is now widely maintained that the controlling focus of Paul's theology, as for Jesus before him, is eschatology—or what is equivalent for some, redemptive history (*historia salutis*). Specifically, the center of his theology has been recognized to be the death and resurrection of Christ in their eschatological significance.

In my view, this basic conclusion is sound and, by now, well established. We have confirmed it here, at least provisionally, in considering the window on Paul's theology provided by 1 Corinthians 15:3–4. Further, it is a conclusion that raises the general question of the relationship between the *historia salutis* and the *ordo salutis* in Paul—or, in more traditional terms, the relationship between the accomplishment and the application of redemption. This question, in turn, carries with it the more specific question as to the place of justification in Paul and how it and other aspects of personal participation in salvation relate to this death-and-resurrection center. Such questions will occupy us further below.

"According to the Scriptures." Returning to 1 Corinthians 15:3–4, it needs to be stressed that the factor of fulfillment indicated there ("according to the Scriptures") is not relative but absolute—consummate. Its finality is nothing less in its proportions than eschatological. Here again I will have to content myself with reviewing broadly and somewhat sketchily matters about which I assume many readers, at least, already have some awareness.

Part of the recent consensus in Pauline scholarship that emerged over the course of the twentieth century, just noted, is that Paul's eschatology has a dual or elliptical focus. For him, the concept of eschatology is to be defined not only in terms of Christ's second coming, by what is still future at his return, but also by his first coming and what has already taken place in Christ, especially his death and resurrection. Paul teaches an eschatology that is, in part, already realized.

In my view, looking over the history of the interpretation of Paul as a whole, the relatively recent pervasive recognition of his realized eschatology represents the truly "new perspective" on Paul, one that is far more important, with wider-ranging implications, than the developments of the past several decades that have been given that designation. My perception is that a commensurate impact of this rediscovery is still to be had in the doctrine and life of the church, in its preaching and teaching. This matter will concern us in greater depth later.

For the purposes of our survey, we may begin with Galatians 1:4. Jesus Christ, "whom God the Father raised from the dead" (v. 1), "gave himself for our sins to rescue us from the present evil age." "For our sins" provides a direct link to 1 Corinthians 15:3 and so to the fulfillment in view there. The expression "the present evil age" reflects Paul's use of the distinction between "this" or "the present age" and "the age to come," a distinction coined in

Second Temple Judaism and taken over from there in the New Testament, but firmly rooted in the Old Testament. Both ages are explicitly mentioned together in Paul only in Ephesians 1:21, but there are numerous references to "this age" elsewhere, as in Galatians 1:4. As such, the two-age construct encompasses consecutively the whole of history from creation to its consummation; the one age follows the other. Given the fall, the entrance of sin and its consequences into the creation, the two ages are also antithetical. This age is the pre-eschatological order, marked by sin, corruption, and death; the age to come is the eschaton of righteousness and life.[7]

According to Galatians 1:4, then, the purpose of Christ's death was nothing less than to deliver the church from the present world order marked by sin and its consequences, and with that deliverance, by implication, to bring believers into the coming world order, the new and final creation marked by eschatological life in all its fullness. The deliverance in view is certainly personal and individual, but it also plainly has corporate and comprehensive, even cosmic and "aeonic" dimensions.

Similar statements occur elsewhere in Paul. For instance, in Colossians 1:13 the outlook on the appropriation of salvation is similarly comprehensive: "He has delivered us from the domain of darkness and transferred us to the kingdom of his beloved Son." Salvation is totalitarian in its dimensions. It consists in being

---

7. The Greek word *aiōn*, particularly as it functions in this construct, has a certain ambivalence. Like the underlying Hebrew *'olam*, originally a comprehensive time word, it takes on as well similarly sweeping spatial connotations and so has the spatio-temporal sense "world-age"; "this *aiōn*" is the present world order of fixed duration. For an older but still helpful treatment of the two-aeon construct in Paul, with some attention to its Second Temple background, see G. Vos, *The Pauline Eschatology* (1930; Grand Rapids: Baker, 1979), ch. 1 ("The Structure of Pauline Eschatology"), 1–41, esp. 36–41. While this construct is based on and faithful to the Old Testament, it first appears in postcanonical materials of the Second Temple period. On balance, as Vos says, "There is no escape from the conclusion that a piece of Jewish theology has been here by Revelation incorporated into the Apostle's teaching" (28 n. 36).

brought out of one dominion into another, from the enslaving regime of sin into the kingdom of Christ with its liberating rule. Back in Galatians 6:14, autobiographic but surely representative for all believers (cf. 2:20), Paul speaks of "the cross of our Lord Jesus Christ, through which *the world* has been crucified to me, and I to *the world*," where "the world" is, in effect, "this world," or "the present evil age" (note the contrasting reference to the "new creation" in v. 15). Here, more clearly than in 1:4, the nothing less than eschatological deliverance effected in the death and resurrection of Christ is an already present reality. In 2 Corinthians 5:17, the "one in Christ" is not simply a "new creature," but is—almost certainly the more accurate translation—of the "new creation." The believer, in union with Christ, is already a participant in God's new and final order for the creation. How, more exactly, this is so will occupy us later.

"For Our Sins." The second factor of significance associated with Christ's death and resurrection in 1 Corinthians 15:3–4, along with eschatological fulfillment, is captured by "for our sins." In view of what we have taken to be the clearly summary nature of this passage and especially in light of what we have just noted about Galatians 1:4, it seems best to take the reference to sin in this phrase comprehensively, as bringing into view sin in all its facets and the totality of its consequences. What further disposes us to this conclusion is the next occurrence of "sins" in the passage (v. 17): absent Christ's resurrection, Paul says to the church, "you are still in your sins." His point here is surely not that they are in their sins only in some respects, say, as sin's corrupting and death-dealing consequences continue, while others, like the guilt incurred, have already been dealt with and removed by his death. Rather, he can only mean "still in your sins" entirely, unrelievedly.

It is surely significant, and not to be missed, that in a centering statement like 1 Corinthians 15:3–4, with its focus on the death and resurrection of Christ, the only other consideration mentioned, along with the fulfillment of Scripture, is sin considered comprehensively. It should come as no surprise, then, that elsewhere in Paul Christ's death is repeatedly seen in relation to sin. In fact, apart from sin and its consequences, Paul sees no place for Christ and his activity. Apart from the sin of Adam—as the first human being from whom all others descend[8]—and its universal repercussions (Rom. 5:12–19), there is no need for the last Adam. "Christ Jesus came into the world to save sinners" (1 Tim. 1:15). This, which is likely another already-existing formulation taken over by Paul, encapsulates for him the agenda for Christ's ministry, specifically the rationale for his death. For Paul, Christology and soteriology are coterminous; he has no Christological interests that are not also soteriological.

In this sense, in terms of a distinction currently in wide use, sin is the "plight," and Christ is the "solution," particularly his being "obedient to death—even death on a cross" (Phil. 2:8). Certainly that plight is made clearer in the light of this solution. But the plight exists apart from the solution and is clear, in fact universally clear, even if suppressed or otherwise denied (Rom. 1:18–20). In other words, the plight, not the solution, is definitive. The plight specifies what the solution must remedy, for which the solution exists and apart from which it is not a solution.

So if we are to understand what Paul says about salvation, including the order of salvation, we must understand what he says about sin. If we are to grasp, at least in an adequate way, what he teaches about Christ's death and resurrection, as well as how the saving benefits effected by them are actually appropriated by sinners, then we must first have an accurate and sufficiently

8. This point is crucial in Paul's theology; for him nothing less than the gospel itself stands or falls with the natural descent of all human beings from Adam and Eve as the first. See esp. J. P. Versteeg, *Adam in the New Testament: Mere Teaching Model or First Historical Man?* (2nd ed., trans. R. B. Gaffin Jr.; Phillipsburg, NJ: P&R, 2012), 9–29, 34–42 (on Paul); cf. ix–xxv.

informed grasp of what he teaches about sin. To put it negatively, the clarity and coherence of Paul's teaching, focused on
Christ's death and resurrection, will never be perceived where
a defective or inadequate understanding of his teaching on sin
is functioning.

This teaching, we should add, is that of Paul the *Christian*.
Only now, in the light of the salvation revealed in Christ and a
corrected reading of the Old Testament, does Paul have a grasp
of sin in its depth and gravity that goes beyond what Saul the
Pharisee (and the Second Temple Judaism he previously exempli-
fied) ever comprehended.

Consequently, it will be worthwhile, even necessary, for us
to give some further attention to Paul's teaching on sin by noting, beyond what we have already seen, its basic profile and key
facets. This is all the more necessary because, while in much
recent discussion there is considerable concentration on Paul's
Christology and his soteriology (the "solution"), particularly its
corporate and ecclesiological dimensions, his understanding of
sin ("the plight") does not receive commensurate and adequate
attention. This is so typically, I would observe, even when the
much-debated issue of the law in Paul is being considered.

Sin[9]

Paul's treatment of sin and its consequences is extensive
and multifaceted, particularly in Romans. Above all, first to
last, sin is theocentric. That is, it is primarily against God and
only then, derivatively, against human beings, including the self
(e.g., Rom. 1:18–32; Eph. 4:17–19). Accordingly, sin is *relational* or,
better, "anti-relational." It is essentially rebellion, an expression
of autonomous revolt against God, the image-bearing (1 Cor.

9. This section utilizes material developed at greater length in my "'The
Scandal of the Cross': Atonement in the Pauline Corpus," in *The Glory of the
Atonement: Essays in Honor of Roger Nicole*, ed. C. E. Hill and F. A. James III
(Downers Grove, IL: InterVarsity Press, 2004), 145–53.

11:7–9) creature's effective renunciation of God as Creator. In the current climate of studying Paul, it is difficult to exaggerate this relational factor, a point to which we will return below. Sin is willful rejection of fellowship with God by refusing to acknowledge him as Creator and to live out of thankful, creaturely dependence on him (Rom. 1:19–21a); it is a deep-seated recoil against the Creator-creature relationship. Inevitably, then, sin is idolatrous, the exchange of "the truth of God for a lie," an exchange that consists, in virtually innumerable ways, in worshiping and serving "the creature rather than the Creator" (1:25). All told, as anti-relational, as flouting and even denying the Creator-creature relationship that nonetheless cannot be escaped, sin is deeply rooted hostility, particularly toward God (Rom. 8:7) and so, again inevitably and in nearly countless ways, also against others and even the self as made in God's image (e.g., 1:26–27, 29–31; Gal. 5:19–21; Eph. 4:19).

As relational in the sense just indicated, sin is also *illegal*, and it is that not simply in addition to or peripheral to its being relational. In its being relational, it is inherently illegal. Its illegality is reflected in the varied vocabulary that Paul uses for sin, most of which has in view what does not accord with God's will or law. "For by the law comes the knowledge of sin," he affirms categorically (Rom. 3:20, ESV; cf. 7:7–13). Like God himself and reflective of his person, "the law is holy, and the commandment is holy, righteous, and good" (Rom. 7:12). It is the law, as the revealed will of God, that identifies and reveals sin. The law is the criterion for sin, the standard by which the likes of pride, rebellion, idolatry, and hostility, as expressions of human autonomy, are sin and manifest themselves as such. An essential and inalienable aspect of sin for Paul is that it is "any want of conformity unto, or transgression of, the law of God" (Westminster Shorter Catechism 14).

It is undoubtedly true that almost always, when Paul refers to "law" or "the law," he has in view the body of legislation given by God through Moses to Israel at Sinai—that legislation marking out the period of covenant history until Christ. He is also clear that, as *a specific codification* belonging to that era, the law has been terminated in its entirety by Christ in his coming (e.g., Rom. 6:14; 7:6; 10:4; 2 Cor. 3:6–11; Gal. 3:17–25). At the same time, however, it seems difficult to deny that in statements like Romans 7:12 (just cited), Romans 13:9 (where several of the Ten Commandments function as exhortation incumbent on the church), and 1 Corinthians 7:19 ("God's commandments"), Paul recognizes that at its moral core, the "Torah in the Torah," as it could be put, the Mosaic law specifies imperatives that transcend the Mosaic economy. Included within that law are imperatives that have been bound up with the indicative of the Creator-creature relationship from the beginning and so are enduring because of who God is. In its central commands, the law given at Sinai, notably the Decalogue, reveals God's will as that which is inherent in his person and therefore incumbent on his image-bearing creatures as such, regardless of time and place, whether Jew or non-Jew.

Sin as relational is thus inherently illegal—the violation of God's will as revealed in Scripture and the creation. This means that sin incurs guilt. Sin, of whatever sort, renders the sinner inalienably guilty before God; nothing is more central to the now-broken relationship between God and the sinner than that guilt.

Sin is also *universal*. Jew as well as non-Jew, "all have sinned" (Rom. 3:23; cf. 3:9, 19), Paul says, reiterating a major conclusion of the first main segment of the argument in Romans (1:18–3:20), which documents the universality of human sin. Sin is universal, not only because every human being actually sins, but also because everyone is a sinner by birth, because everyone enters the world with an inherited disposition to sin, which is itself sinful and therefore culpable. This, I take it, without arguing it here, is surely one of his points in the Archimedean-like passage, Romans 5:12–19. To say, as do some, that Paul "does believe in

Original Sin, but not Original Guilt,"[10] introduces a disjunction the apostle would never recognize. Paul knows of no sin, whether imputed, inborn disposition, or actual commission, that does not entail guilt and judicial liability for its consequences.

Sin is not only rebellion against God and violation of his law, but also an *enslaving and corrupting power*. This aspect of sin is captured, most emphatically in Romans 6–7, by personifying it as a lord or master. Correlatively, the sinner is a slave, in bondage to sin (e.g., 6:6, 12, 14, 16–20, 22). Elsewhere (Eph. 2:1, 5; Col. 2:13), the unrelieved desperation of this slavery is expressed as being nothing less than "dead in . . . transgressions and sins," a deadness that manifests itself as corrupt living ("walking") in submission to Satan as "the ruler of the kingdom of the air" (Eph. 2:2). Further—and this should not be missed, as it ties in with what we have already seen—in this deadness and corruption, sinners are as culpable as they are helpless. They are "by nature children of wrath" (2:3; cf. 5:6; Col. 3:6).

Sin elicits God's wrath. As more careful study of Paul will show, divine wrath is neither an impersonal process nor a merely reflexive abandoning of sinners to the baleful but penultimate, inner-worldly consequences of their sinning. Rather, God's wrath is his active recoil against sin, a positive recoil that arises from concerns of his person, especially his holiness and justice, such that it finds its ultimate expression, necessarily judicially punitive and retributive in view of those concerns, in death as the eternal destruction of sinners. This is indisputable from statements like Romans 2:8, 1 Thessalonians 1:10, 2 Thessalonians 2:10, 12, and especially 2 Thessalonians 1:6, 8–9. For Paul, human death in all its dimensions[11] is penal and essentially punitive.

10. D. E. H. Whiteley, *The Theology of St. Paul* (Oxford: Blackwell, 1964), 51, quoted with approval by J. D. G. Dunn, *The Theology of Paul the Apostle* (Grand Rapids: Eerdmans, 1998), 97 n. 81.

11. Entirely alien to Paul is any notion that biological human death is a natural phenomenon inherent to being human and not the consequence of human sin, specifically the sin of Adam as the first human being from whom

Sin has all sorts of disastrous and ruinous consequences. Its destructive and horrendous results are multiple and virtually incalculable, as shown, for instance, by the extensive, unrelieved detailing at the end of Romans 1. It is important to recognize, however, that all these ramifications involve a basic, irreducible, twofold consequence. In terms of the relationship between God and sinners, one consequence primarily pertains to God and the concerns of his person. The other basic consequence primarily concerns sinners and their constitution or makeup as persons. These twin consequences are guilt and enslavement. Sin renders sinners both inexcusably guilty and helplessly enslaved.

This, as Paul sees it, is the grim "plight" of sinners, a plight that is all the more grim because left to themselves sinners are unable to comprehend adequately, much less acknowledge, either their guilt or the bondage of their corruption. Even less can they grasp what the solution is. This inability is clearly pointed out in 1 Corinthians 2:14. The unbeliever "does not accept the things of the Spirit of God, for . . . he cannot understand them." Inevitably, then, the only remedy, the cross, is "foolishness" and a "scandal" to all unbelievers, Jew and non-Jew alike (1 Cor. 1:18–23). But it is just sinners like these, "dead in their transgressions and sins" and "children of wrath, like the rest," that God, "being rich in mercy," has "loved" with his "great love," his great saving love revealed in Christ (Eph. 2:3–4).

Returning again to 1 Corinthians 15:3–4, with its centering focus, the phrase "for our sins" is properly understood in terms of this basic and irreducible dual profile of sin. The efficacy of the cross, together with the resurrection, is that it destroys sin, both guilt for sin and slavery to sin, and it does that only as it eradicates them together, though not in the same way. As that is the case, so correspondingly Christ's death, together with his resurrection, as it is "for sin" comprehensively, addresses both

---

all other human beings have descended and are justly implicated in his sin. See Versteeg, *Adam in the New Testament*, 9–29, 34–42, 53–67; cf. x–xxv.

the sinner's status and his constitution. The efficacy of Christ's death and resurrection, applied to the sinner, is forensic as well as re-creational and transformative. Involved, in other words, as we will consider more carefully below, is not only justification but also sanctification. Related benefits like adoption and reconciliation are also to be distinguished, accounted for, and understood in terms of this irreducible, twofold distinction between the forensic and the re-creational.

So when Paul says concerning the gospel, at its center, "Christ died for our sins," he surely has justification in view, as Romans 4:25, the culmination of his argument to that point, highlights: "delivered up for our sins . . . raised for our justification." But sanctification, no less than justification, is given with this gospel center. In that regard, 2 Corinthians 5:15 is quite clear: "he died for all [i.e., as sinners, "for their sins"], that those who live might no longer live for themselves but for him who died and was raised for them [for their sake, on their behalf]."

It is worth noting at this point that because of the way Paul focuses the gospel on Christ's death and resurrection in their unified efficacy, without at all confusing justification and sanctification, the forensic and renovative aspects of salvation, he sees them together more easily and inseparably than is sometimes the case in the Reformation tradition—including, in my perception, many evangelical circles today. For example, several years ago I was listening to a conference tape where the speaker said this (I believe I have transcribed his words exactly, adding punctuation and italics): "What Christ has done *for* us *is* Christianity; what he does *in* us is his own business, but what he's done for us is Christianity. The Reformers really believed, and their followers really believed, that *nothing that happens in me is the gospel*; nothing that happens in me is the gospel. The gospel is external. It has to do with Christ dying for me."

One must certainly appreciate the concern of this speaker, which, if I heard him correctly, was that the truth of the gospel not be lost in a sea of subjective experience. But his statement is not one that Paul would make, for it significantly abridges and so distorts the scope of his *gospel*, the scope of the Pauline "for us." And, I would be prepared to argue, with some emphasis, it distorts the outlook of the Reformation, at least in its best and not untypical representatives.

Union with Christ

In our summary probe of the center of Paul's theology, there is another factor that needs to be noted, the union of Christians with Christ. While that union lies beyond the explicit terms of 1 Corinthians 15:3–4, it is of paramount importance for Paul, absolutely decisive for what falls within the purview of matters "of first importance."

Paul's understanding of union with Christ, to provide a brief sketch, stems from the Old Testament and, as much as anything, shows him to be a covenant theologian. There, in the Old Testament, the bond between God and Israel, as his covenant people, is expressed in a variety of ways, but perhaps most evocatively in the description of God himself as "the portion" of his people (Pss. 73:26; 119:57; Jer. 10:16). Reciprocally, they are "the Lord's portion" (Deut. 32:9). Particularly noteworthy in this regard is Isaiah 53:12, which speaks of the Lord's anointed servant, the one who, among other things, was "wounded for our transgressions" and "crushed for our iniquities" (v. 5).[12] As the reward for those sufferings, the Lord says, "I will allot him a portion with the many."[13]

The climactic realization of this covenantal bond, this reciprocal possession between the triune God and his people, the

12. It is difficult not to see "for our iniquities" here as underlying "for our sins/transgressions" in 1 Cor. 15:3 and Rom. 4:25.

13. Here *rabbim* is appropriately read as "the many" (ESV), rather than, with most translations, "the great" (plural); see the Septuagint, *autos klēronomēsei pollous*, "he shall inherit many."

church, is centered for Paul in union with Christ. This, as we will have occasion to see, is the central truth of salvation for Paul, the key soteriological reality comprising all others. While the phrase "union with Christ" does not occur in Paul (or elsewhere in the New Testament), the reality is described in various ways and is particularly prominent in his use of the prepositional phrase "in Christ/the Lord" with other slight variations, particularly involving the preposition "with." Scholarly debate about the phrase's meaning has often focused on the force of the preposition "in" (*en*) and views range from a purely instrumental understanding to a local or atmospheric sense and even the notion of an actual physical union between Christ and believers.[14]

In fact, Paul's usage is varied. Something of its full scope may be gauged by the contrast between Adam and Christ, as the second or last Adam (Rom. 5:12–19; 1 Cor. 15:21–22, 45, 47). What each does is determinative—in fact, decisive for life and death, respectively—for those who are "in him" as their representative and, in the case of Christ, as their substitute in propitiating the just wrath that their sins deserve (e.g., Rom. 3:25–26).[15] In this respect, the terms "for us" and "for our sins" correlate with, and are inseparable from, the terms "in him" and "with him"; the former function only within the bond indicated by the latter. At the same time, "for us" signals the uniqueness of Christ and what is irreversible and noninterchangeable within this bond. That could hardly be made clearer than by the rhetorical question in 1 Corinthians 1:13, "Was Paul crucified for you?"

For those who are "in Christ," this union or solidarity is all-encompassing, extending in fact from eternity to eternity, from what is true of them "before the creation of the world"

14. For a thorough and careful overall treatment, see the recent work of C. R. Campbell, *Paul and Union with Christ: An Exegetical and Theological Study* (Grand Rapids: Zondervan, 2012).

15. To see Christ as a representative, especially as no more than an example, but not also as a substitute, seriously distorts Paul's understanding.

(Eph. 1:4, 9) to their still future glorification (Rom. 8:17; 1 Cor. 15:22). Accordingly, to see the concept of union with Christ as crucial for Paul is hardly an alien imposition on him or an undue systematizing or schematizing. Rather, it promotes needed clarity to recognize a threefold categorical distinction. His "in Christ" is either (1) *predestinarian* (Eph. 1:4), (2) *past* or *redemptive-historical*—the union involved in the once-for-all accomplishment of salvation, particularly in Christ's death and resurrection, or (3) *present*, looking forward to Christ's return—union in the actual possession or application of salvation, and in that sense *existential* union.

These distinctions, it should not be missed, point not to different unions, but to different aspects or dimensions of a single union. At the same time, it is essential to recognize each of these dimensions and to do so without equivocating, either by denying any one of them or by blurring the distinction between them. The need for such distinguishing can be illustrated by an instructive example that is directly pertinent to our primary concern, applicatory or actual (present) union.

In Romans 16:7, Paul mentions those who "were in Christ before me" or "before I was." Here Paul, speaking autobiographically, but surely representatively for all Christians, points to a critical, before-and-after transition in being "in Christ." Within the overall context of his teaching, Paul knows himself to have been chosen "in Christ" from eternity ("before the foundation of the world," Eph. 1:4) and also to have been contemplated "with him" at the time of his death and resurrection ("in the fullness of time," Gal. 4:4). Nonetheless, there was still a time in his life, during his pre-Christian past, when he was "outside" of Christ in the sense he speaks of here, a time when he was, personalizing the plural in Ephesians 2:3, "a child of wrath, like the rest." Here an absolutely crucial question, an *ordo salutis* question, emerges. What effects this transition from wrath to grace, from the wrath of being "outside" Christ to salvation from that wrath by being "in Christ"? This, as much as any, is the key question before us, one that will occupy us until we arrive at the answer.

Focusing now particularly on present union, union in the actual appropriation or application of salvation, the *ordo salutis* aspect of union, several facets may be noted. In addition to its continuing, as do predestinarian and redemptive-historical union, to be *representative* and *legal*, it now becomes *mystical*. That is so in the sense of involving "a great mystery" that for Paul apparently has its closest analogy in the relationship between husband and wife (Eph. 5:32).

This analogy certainly points to the deep intimacy of the union involved. But at the same time it keeps clear an important consideration. Such intimacy, however sublime, does not remove or even blur the personal distinction between Christ and the Christian. The personal identity of each is maintained. "Mystical" union does not efface or otherwise compromise personal integrity. This means that in present union Christ retains his representative and substitutionary role. This role is perhaps most climactically evident in his present intercession for believers "at the right hand of God" (Rom. 8:34).

In this regard, it is hardly helpful, and will only serve to distort Paul's teaching, to think in terms of two unions in the application of redemption, one legal and representative, and the other mystical and spiritual in the sense of being renovative. That viewpoint, understandably and properly concerned that the difference between the legal and the renovative (i.e., justification and sanctification) not be blurred or otherwise compromised, loses the integral unity of Paul's outlook. There is but one union, with distinguishable but inseparable, coexisting legal and renovative aspects.

Present union is also *spiritual*. This is so, not in an immaterial, idealistic sense, but because of the activity and indwelling of the Holy Spirit. This gives to present union with Christ its distinctiveness. It also circumscribes the mystery involved and protects against confusing it with other kinds of union. Since it is effected by the Holy Spirit, present union is neither ontological (like that between the persons of the Trinity), nor hypostatic (like that between Christ's divine and human natures), nor psychosomatic (between body and soul in human personality), nor somatic (between husband and wife)—nor is it merely intellectual and moral, a unity in understanding, affections, and purpose.

Spiritual union stems from the relationship between Christ and the Holy Spirit given with Christ's glorification and lying in back of this union. This consideration is fundamental for Paul, and some of its implications will occupy us later. Here we may briefly note that because of his resurrection and ascension, the incarnate Christ ("the last Adam") has been so transformed by the Spirit and is now in such complete possession of the Spirit that he has "become life-giving Spirit," with the result that now "the Lord [= the exalted Christ] is the Spirit" (1 Cor. 15:45; 2 Cor. 3:17).[16]

In view is a functional equation that does not efface personal distinction, a oneness in their activity of giving resurrection life (1 Cor. 15) and eschatological freedom (2 Cor. 3), so that, in the life of the church and within believers, Christ and the Spirit are inseparable—in fact, one. So, for example, in Romans 8:9–10, "you in the Spirit," "the Spirit in you," you "belonging to Christ" or "of Christ" (close, perhaps equivalent, to "in Christ"), and "Christ in you" are all inseparable facets describing a single union. Likewise, in Ephesians 3:16–17, to have "his Spirit in your inner man" is for "Christ . . . [to] dwell in your hearts."

Accordingly, being Spiritual—and there is some value in capitalizing the adjective, at least mentally, to keep clear that the activity of the Holy Spirit is in view and to guard against

16. For an extended discussion of these and related passages, see my "The Last Adam, the Life-Giving Spirit," in *The Forgotten Christ: Exploring the Majesty and Mystery of God Incarnate*, ed. S. Clark (Nottingham: Apollos, 2007), 191–231, and "'Life-Giving Spirit': Probing the Center of Paul's Pneumatology," *Journal of the Evangelical Theological Society* 41.4 (December 1998): 573–89, as well as the supporting literature cited in both articles.

unbiblical notions of an idealistic and immaterial substance being involved—present union has a *reciprocal* character. Not only are believers in Christ, but he also is in them—indeed, "the hope of glory" for the church is "Christ in you" (Col. 1:27). Such union, then, is also inherently *vital*. Christ's indwelling by the Spirit is the very life of the believer: "I no longer live, but Christ lives in me" (Gal. 2:20); "your life is hid with Christ in God" (Col. 3:4).

Finally, present union is *indissoluble*. This follows from its being rooted in election "in [Christ] before the foundation of the world" (Eph. 1:4). The salvation eternally purposed for believers "in Christ" is infallibly certain of reaching its eschatological consummation in their bodily resurrection and glorification "in Christ" (e.g., Rom. 8:17; 1 Cor. 15:20, 23).

To sum up: present union with Christ—sharing with him in all he has accomplished and now is, by virtue of his death and resurrection—is, as much as anything, at the center of Paul's soteriology.[17]

Union and Justification

This major conclusion prompts some initial observations on the relationship in Paul between relational or participatory concerns and legal, forensic concerns—or, as it has been put most recently, between his "participationist" and his "juristic" interests (E. P. Sanders).[18] Specifically at issue is how Paul views the relationship between union and justification.

---

17. For a particularly helpful discussion of union with Christ, see J. Murray, *Redemption Accomplished and Applied* (Grand Rapids: Eerdmans, 1955), 201–13. In my comments here, I have utilized categories from this discussion as well as Murray's classroom lectures; see also, reflecting on Murray's discussion, my "Union with Christ: Some Biblical and Theological Reflections," in *Always Reforming: Explorations in Systematic Theology*, ed. A. T. B. McGowan (Downers Grove, IL: IVP Academic, 2006), 271–88. My discussion above utilizes material found on pages 272–75.

18. See, e.g., E. P. Sanders, *Paul and Palestinian Judaism: A Comparison of Patterns of Religion* (London: SCM, 1977), 502–8, 519–20.

On the question of this relationship, a couple of fairly wide-spread tendencies are observable in the modern period. The first is to distinguish union and justification as two strands of teaching in Paul that either are in tension or are simply coexisting but separable interests. Or they are seen as interchangeable or optional metaphors for the same reality. This has most often worked out to the depreciation of the forensic, as in Schweitzer's well-known description of justification as a "subsidiary crater" in the "main crater" of Paul's theology as a whole.[19] This tendency is often bound up with a second one, the tendency to equate union and the participatory with concerns having to do exclusively with renewal and personal renovation and the subduing of sin as an enslaving power.

This way of viewing things, it can hardly be overemphasized, has been the source of considerable confusion. In Paul, answering to the fully relational liability of sin as guilt, noted above, the relational and legal concerns in salvation, the participatory and the forensic, belong together. The participatory or relational involves an inalienable legal, forensic aspect, and the forensic does not function apart from, but always within, the participatory. This means that Paul's relational-participatory teaching surely includes, but may not simply be equated with, the renovative ("Christ in me," understood in that sense), as distinct or even somehow separable from the forensic ("Christ for me").

Rather, both, the forensic and the transformative, justification and sanctification, are functions or manifestations of the relational. Expressed concretely, both are manifestations or aspects of union with Christ. Christ "in us" continues to be, and is as such also, Christ "for us." In union with us, Christ has a significance that is decisively forensic as well as powerfully transforming. This is obviously a fundamental consideration, one that will occupy us in some detail in the next two chapters.

19. A. Schweitzer, *The Mysticism of Paul the Apostle* (ET; New York: H. Holt, 1931), 225.

The Role of Faith

With union with Christ in view, and still with an eye to the center of Paul's theology, this is a good place to say something more about faith (something of its decisive role was already noted toward the beginning of this chapter). Particularly important is the essential role of faith in being united to Christ. At stake in Paul's gospel in 1 Corinthians 15, is whether or not those who have "received" the gospel "have believed in vain" (v. 2). Accented further here is believing ("receiving") as involving "standing in" (v. 1) and "holding fast" (v. 2) the gospel. This persevering faith in the gospel is manifestly faith in Christ (*pistis eis Christon*) and as such, as entrusting oneself to him, one is united to him. Faith for Paul is the bond of that union, viewed from the side of the one united with Christ (Eph. 3:17).[20]

Faith unites to Christ, so that his death and resurrection are mine, in the sense of now being savingly effective in my life. Better, faith is the work of God by his Spirit, effective in "calling" sinners—otherwise "dead in trespasses and sins" (Eph. 2:1, 5) and thus utterly incapable of faith in and of themselves—"into the fellowship of his Son" (1 Cor. 1:9), into union with Christ, who is what he now is as crucified and resurrected. This union with the exalted Christ is such that his death and resurrection in their saving efficacy from sin and all its consequences—that is, basically, from its guilt and power—are mine. Or, put even more elementally and integrally, by union with the exalted Christ, all that he now is and has secured for believers by virtue of having been crucified and raised is mine, whether presently or in the future.

An important caveat of sorts needs to be made at this point, especially in view of the current preoccupation of some New Perspective proponents with the corporate dimensions of Paul's

---

20. Calvin, for one, has captured this Pauline understanding well in *Institutes*, 1:537–38 (3.1.1).

theology, including what is perceived to be the predominantly, if not exclusively, ecclesiological concern of his teaching on justification. What has been said above about faith and union with Christ has been put in personal, individual terms. That has been done deliberately because this personal aspect runs the risk of becoming eclipsed in the present climate of preoccupation with the corporate, but also because it is so vital for Paul. Note, to cite just a couple of examples, the personal, individual accent, autobiographic but surely true for every believer, in Galatians 2:20, "who loved me and gave himself for me," and 1 Timothy 1:13, 15, "I . . . a blasphemer, a persecutor, and an insolent man . . . chief of sinners . . . obtained mercy."

But now this caveat. This emphasis on the individual and personal is not meant to deny or downplay the broader corporate, even cosmic, dimensions of the salvation revealed in the cross and resurrection and appropriated by faith. The call into fellowship with Christ (1 Cor. 1:9) is also a call into the fellowship of his Spirit-baptized body (12:13). The bodies of believers are, individually, temples of the Holy Spirit (1 Cor. 6:19; cf. 1 Thess. 4:6, 8), while the church itself, as a whole, is God's temple (1 Cor. 3:16–17). Further, that is so in the context of the entire creation "anxiously longing" for the future (open) "revelation of the sons of God," when it will be "set free from the bondage of corruption" (Rom. 8:19, 21). To polarize personal and corporate, or personal and cosmic, concerns in matters of the gospel is simply foreign to Paul. So is allowing either one to eclipse or negate the other.[21]

---

21. Contra, e.g., D. VanDrunen, *Living in God's Two Kingdoms: A Biblical Vision for Christianity and Culture* (Wheaton, IL: Crossway, 2010), 65–66, in the course of arguing from Rom. 8:18–23 that "Our earthly bodies are the only part of the present world that Scripture says will be transformed and taken up into the world-to-come. *Believers themselves* are the point of continuity between this creation and the new creation" (66, italics original).

To say nothing further here, it hardly does justice to the terms of v. 21 to say, as he does on the same page, that "the resurrection of believers is the focal point of creation's longing (8:19, 21, 23)." That is indeed true, but the focus of

The Center of Paul's Theology and the Order of Salvation

Our reflections tethered to the center of Paul's theology, with an eye to the question of how in Paul salvation is actually applied to and received by the individual sinner, have brought us to this overall conclusion: the central soteriological reality is union with the exalted Christ by Spirit-created faith. That is the nub, the essence, of the way or order of salvation for Paul.

The center of Paul's soteriology, then, at the center of his theology as a whole, is neither justification by faith nor sanctification, neither the imputation of Christ's righteousness nor the renewing work of the Spirit. To draw that conclusion, however, is not to decenter justification (or sanctification), as if justification is somehow less important for Paul than it is for the Reformers. Justification is supremely important; it is absolutely crucial in Paul's "gospel of salvation" (cf. Eph. 1:13). If his teaching on justification is denied or distorted, it ceases to be gospel; there is no longer saving "good news" for guilty sinners. But no matter how close justification is to the heart of Paul's gospel, in our salvation there is an antecedent consideration, a reality that is deeper, more fundamental, more decisive, more crucial: Christ and our union with him, the crucified and resurrected, the exalted, Christ. Union with Christ by faith—that is the essence of Paul's *ordo salutis*.[22]

---

creation's longing includes as well its distinct and inseparable "expectation" (v. 19) "that the creation itself will be set free from its bondage to decay and obtain the freedom of the glory of the children of God" (ESV). This being "set free" and correlative "obtaining," or being "brought into" (NIV)—fair renderings of the Greek text—can hardly be construed, as VanDrunen does, as amounting to the annihilation of the present creation with the sole exception of believers.

22. To speak of the "essence" of a matter is obviously not to be making a statement about it in its entirety. My point is not that in Paul union with Christ is all there is to the application of salvation, with no further differentiations or delineation. That is certainly not the case. Clearly, he distinguishes justification from sanctification and both from union, and he is concerned with the relationships among them. My comments above and elsewhere in no way mean to suggest that issues addressed in conventional discussions of

At the opening of Book 3 of his *Institutes of the Christian Religion* and controlling all that he has to say about "the way" of salvation—that is, its personal, individual appropriation, including what he will eventually say about justification—Calvin writes, "First, we must understand that as long as Christ remains outside of us, and we are separated from him, all that he has suffered and done for the salvation of the human race remains useless and of no value for us."[23] This is eminently faithful to Paul and is quoted here because it captures the essence of his soteriology.

Justification in the Order of Salvation

As we have seen, the salvation appropriated in union with Christ, by faith, consists of two basic, irreducible facets. These facets answer to sin's two basic consequences; one facet is forensic, the other, renovative. More specifically, in Paul these two facets are instanced by justification and sanctification. To this point, I have largely asserted, rather than argued or demonstrated, this basic profile for justification and sanctification and that they are to be distinguished in terms of it.

So far as sanctification is concerned, there is probably little, if any, dispute about its renovative character. Paul's teaching on justification, however, is quite another matter. Considerable controversy presently swirls around it. Here I will not become involved in this debate in any extensive way. That would require a book of its own, and the focus of this book, though related to this debate, is somewhat different. However, in the interest of further exploring our focus and also with an eye to the ongoing debates, it may be useful at this juncture to make, as they appear to me, some baseline observations about justification in Paul.

---

the *ordo salutis* are somehow out of place for the study of Paul. Certainly, in addition to what has just been noted, he is clear, and it is important for him to be clear, that justification is logically as well as chronologically (though not causally) prior to sanctification as an ongoing process in the life of the believer.

23. Calvin, *Institutes*, 1:537 (3.1.1).

First, in terms of the current debates, sparked as they are largely by certain New Perspective conclusions, I remain unpersuaded that the Reformation and the Reformation tradition have gotten it wrong and that, for Paul, justification is at least primarily, if not entirely, about ecclesiology rather than soteriology—about whom you may eat with and are to have fellowship as a Christian, rather than how you become a Christian. On this view—primarily for some of its proponents, exclusively for others—Paul's teaching on justification, especially in Galatians, is definitive for being and living as a Christian, rather than for becoming a Christian.

For Paul, justification undoubtedly has ecclesiological implications, and these are a prominent concern, especially in Galatians. These implications must not be denied, obscured, or downplayed through an unduly individualistic soteriological mind-set. No doubt, too, they have not always been appreciated as they should. But justification in Paul is essentially and primarily soteriological. It is a "transfer" term, describing what takes place in an individual's transition from wrath to grace, a component of what is effected at the point of being "delivered from the domain of darkness and transferred into the kingdom of his beloved Son" (Col. 1:13).

Even in Galatians, Paul's teaching on justification has its stark urgency, but not simply because church unity is at stake. His rebuke of Peter's conduct is so unsparing, not just because unity between Jew and Gentile is being jeopardized, but because of what that broken unity is symptomatic, because he sees that such conduct strikes at "the truth of the gospel" (2:14). Moreover, it conflicts with that gospel truth because the gospel, as he expresses it programmatically elsewhere, is not the reflex, *post facto*, of having been saved. Rather, it is "the power of God *unto* salvation" (Rom. 1:16), or even more tersely, "the gospel of your salvation" (Eph. 1:13).

This deeply soteriological intention and thrust of his teaching, primarily in Romans and Galatians, that justification is by grace and so by faith and not by (the) works (of the law) is put beyond question, I take it, from later and more generalized assertions that Paul makes. In Ephesians 2:8–9, it is salvation, not justification, that is "by grace through faith, and not by works." Here "having been saved" is most likely comprehensive, including every blessing given at the initiation of salvation. Salvation is not limited to, but certainly includes, being justified. At the very least, considering this passage, the two are parallel, in that they are effected in the same way. It would be exceedingly implausible to maintain that here "by faith, not by works" describes soteriological transfer for Paul, as it plainly does, but does not describe it also in his teaching on justification in Romans and Galatians.

Similarly, in Titus 3:5–7, what is excluded for salvation is "works done in righteousness," and further, the effecting of that *salvation* is explicated in part as "having been justified by . . . grace." To the same intent 2 Timothy 1:9, states that God "has saved us . . . not according to our works, but according to his own purpose and grace." Unless there are compelling considerations to the contrary, which so far have not been offered, Paul's opposition between faith and works in Galatians and Romans ought to be read in light of, or at least in continuity with, the generalized soteriological antitheses of these latter passages.

One reason these passages have not received the attention they should in current discussions is that the Pauline authorship of Ephesians and the Pastoral Epistles is widely denied by New Perspective proponents. But even if we grant that denial for the sake of argument, that would still mean that already in the earliest post-Pauline generation of the church, including the sphere of Paul's particular influence, from which Ephesians and the Pastorals stem, according to many who deny their Pauline authorship, the primary point of his teaching on justification in Galatians and Romans, according to the New Perspective, was missed or misunderstood. Providing a plausible historical explanation for such a state of affairs is, to say the least, difficult.

As a second baseline consideration, while Paul's teaching on justification can no doubt be approached from a number of angles, it seems to me that if we ask what brings us to its deepest level, where we find the most fundamental theological considerations shaping and controlling that teaching, that entry point would be the contrasting parallelism between Adam and Christ in Romans 5 and 1 Corinthians 15.

Although this is often overlooked, the terms of the contrast are not the same in both passages, and those differences need to be appreciated. In Romans 5:12–21 (and 1 Corinthians 15:21–22), the contrast is between the Adam of Genesis 3, the fallen sinner, and Christ as righteous; Adam's death-dealing transgression stands in opposition to Christ's obedience and reconciling death (vv. 5–10, esp. 10). In 1 Corinthians 15:45–49, this contrast, already sweeping enough in Romans 5, is even broader, between Adam as *created*, the Adam of Genesis 2 before the fall,[24] and Christ as resurrected, the bearer of resurrection, eschatological life, as life-giving Spirit in the sense of the Holy Spirit, as noted earlier.

What needs especially to be appreciated here is the full sweep of this contrast in 1 Corinthians 15:45–49. It provides an angle of vision that in its breadth is, so far as I can see, along with Colossians 1:15–18, unique in the Pauline corpus. That breadth can be seen from the way in which Adam and Christ are identified as representatives or key figures in solidarity with others. The order of Paul's outlook here is such that Adam is "the first" (*ho prōtos*, v. 45); there is no one *before* him. Christ is "the last" (*ho eschatos*); there is no one *after* him; he is literally *the eschatological man*.

But Christ is not only "the last," but also "the second" (*ho deuteros*, v. 47); there is no one *between* Adam and him. In other words, and this is particularly important for us here, the sweep of Paul's covenant-historical outlook, the overarching hierarchy of his concerns here, is such that no one comes into consideration but Adam and Christ—not David, not Moses and the

---

24. Note the citation of Gen. 2:7 in v. 45.

law given at Sinai, not even Abraham as the promise holder, not Noah, nor anyone else. Fairly utilizing the language of Romans 5:14 here in 1 Corinthians 15, Adam is the "type" or "pattern" (*typos*) of "the one to come," Christ, and of *no one in between*. As Paul is looking at things in this passage, no one else between them "counts."

The narrative line Paul sketches here is such, as it could be put, that "Israel's story" falls below that line. Israel's history is beneath the horizon in view here. Better, within the overall context of Paul's theology, Israel's story in its unfolding subserves the larger, universal story, that larger covenant history that is here given its ultimate profiling: creation and the new creation, the original creation and its consummation, each beginning with and determined by an Adam of its own.

It is from this mega-perspective, then, that Paul's statements on justification in Romans 5:12–21, explicit in terms of the Adam-Christ contrast, will have to be considered and as, accordingly, they specify basic dimensions of his teaching on justification as a whole. These dimensions, we may say, are truly "timeless," not in the sense of being ahistorical, of having their meaning and validity above time and history, but of being perennial and enduring, of not being tied to issues of particular times or ethnicities. Perhaps we could speak of these dimensions as transhistorical and "transethnic" in the sense that they have their ultimate point of reference in Adam's sin and its basic consequences for all of humanity, regardless of ethnicity, throughout its history.

Certainly these dimensions are antecedent in covenant history to Israel's ethnicity and also deeper than issues raised by Israel in relation to other nations. This observation counters a widespread New Perspective emphasis. Paul's doctrine of justification, seen at its deepest level of concern, including its opposition between faith and (the) works (of the law), is not, at least first of all, about the unity in Christ of Jew and Gentile. That unity, as crucial and as integral an outcome of the gospel as it is, is but a primary ecclesiological epiphenomenon emanating from the soteriological core of that doctrine.

In this light, several further observations may be made about Romans 5:12–21:

One. Within the controlling antithetical parallelism, the flow of thought is along two axes: from sin to condemnation to death, on the one side; on the other, from righteousness/obedience to justification to life. Note how this antithetical correspondence matches up with its opposite at each of the three points on these two axes: sin and righteousness, condemnation and justification, death and life.

Two. Righteousness, realized in and constituted by Christ's work, answers to sin. While righteousness surely has its place within the relationship of which he is the head and representative, it is not itself a relational reality or concept—a characteristic New Perspective misconception. Rather, it has a relational aspect as it has its sense in antithesis to sin as trespass of the divine will and, positively, as it consists in obedience to that will.

Three. Justification, the consequence in view of Christ's righteousness, answers to condemnation. In other words, as condemnation is plainly forensic and declarative, so justification is likewise forensic and declarative, and it is forensic specifically as it redresses and removes the guilt and condemnation resulting from sin. Justification is not renovative, nor is it inclusive of renovation. Nor is it an alternative metaphor for being transformed, whether personally, corporately, or cosmically. It is not based on renewal, but exclusively on Christ's righteousness and obedience. Negatively considered, justification is acquittal, the "not guilty" verdict reversing the condemnation of the sinner; it is the forgiveness of sins as the nonreckoning of sin (cf. 4:7–8). Positively considered, it is the declaration, the judicial reckoning, that the sinner is righteous.

This forensic transaction is in view, I take it, not in all, but in the large majority of Paul's uses of the corresponding verb (*dikaioō*), which have a transitive-active, not a stative force. As such, this usage involves the notion of judicial reckoning or imputation. This is so, regardless of how often or how seldom the language of imputation is explicit in Paul.

Also, justification undoubtedly has a corporate concern and important communal implications. But these exist only as individual sinners, each of "the ungodly," are justified, by faith, in the sense just indicated.

Four. Life, answering antithetically to death and as the eschatological life revealed in Christ's resurrection, destroys death and does so depending on how we are to take "justification of life" (*dikaiōsin zōēs*) in verse 18—whether life is in view as the consequence of justification or, alternatively, as its de facto revelation. That Christ "was raised for our justification" (Rom. 4:25), as the event of his own de facto justification, supports the latter sense, but does not exclude the former.

Third and finally, the preceding reflections prompt some additional comments on the relationship between justification and union with Christ. Certainly for Paul, justification takes place in union with Christ. There is no justification apart from that union. That is clearly pointed up in Galatians 2:17, "seeking to be justified in Christ," and in Philippians 3:8–9, where justification, in view "as not having a righteousness of my own that comes from the law, but which comes through faith in Christ," flows from "gaining Christ and being found in him."

Here is a consideration that has sometimes not been adequately appreciated in the Reformation tradition, where a tendency is observable to conceive of or at least treat justification as a stand-alone imputative act. Unless I need to be corrected, this is more the case in the Lutheran tradition, where in the *ordo salutis* union is regularly sequenced following justification, as a fruit or consequence of justification.[25] The Reformed tradition has recognized better and more clearly that, as answer 69 of the Westminster Larger Catechism puts it, justification is among the benefits that "manifest" that union.[26]

But what about imputation? As Paul sees it, does union, as justifying, leave no place for imputation? Does union, as it has been put, make imputation "redundant"?[27] In addition to factors, already noted, that point to an effective or transactional reckoning that amounts to imputation, there is also this to consider in the light of Paul's teaching. Union with Christ, as already noted, does not destroy the personal distinction between him and the believer. The "in him" does not cancel out the "for us/me" that Christ remains just for those in union with him. There is a very real sense in which in union with Christ, Christ remains "outside" of the believer.[28]

What, then, is the ground of the justification that is mine in union with Christ, the basis of my being justified in him? There

25. See, e.g., J. T. Mueller, *Christian Dogmatics* (St. Louis: Concordia, 1934), 320, 381; F. Pieper, *Christian Dogmatics* (St. Louis: Concordia, 1951, 1953), 2:410, 434 n. 65; 3:8 n. 9, 398; see also the survey volume of H. Schmid, *The Doctrinal Theology of the Evangelical Lutheran Church* (3rd rev. ed.; Minneapolis: Augsburg, 1961), 481ff. These materials, taken as representative of mainstream Lutheran orthodoxy from the 17th to the 20th centuries, clearly express the point made about them above. Note that nothing is being said here about Luther's own views on the relationship between union and justification.

26. "The communion in grace which the members of the invisible church have with Christ, is their partaking of the virtue of his mediation, in their justification, adoption, sanctification, and whatever else, in this life, manifests their union with him"; the same pattern of application, with union prior to justification, is present in Westminster Shorter Catechism 30–32.

27. R. Lusk, "A Response to 'The Biblical Plan of Salvation,'" in *The Auburn Avenue Theology, Pros and Cons*, ed. E. C. Beisner (Fort Lauderdale, FL: Knox Theological Seminary, 2004), 118–48, at p. 142.

28. Cf. Calvin, *Institutes*, 1:741 (3.11.11, last sentence).

would appear to be only three conceivable options in reading Paul: (1) Christ's own righteousness, complete and finished in his obedience, culminating on the cross, the righteousness that he now is and embodies in his exaltation (1 Cor. 1:30); (2) the union itself, the fact of the relationship, the existence of the uniting bond as such; or (3) the righteousness and obedience being produced by the transforming work of the Spirit in those who are in union with Christ. In short, in union with Christ the ground of justification is resident either (1) in Christ as distinct from the believer, (2) in the uniting bond itself between Christ and the believer, or (3) in the believer as distinct from Christ.

It appears that the current readiness to dispense with imputation stems from taking, whether or not intentionally, either of the latter two options just mentioned as, in effect, the ground of justification. But neither is sustainable. The relationship as such, no matter how real and intimate, distinct from the persons in that relationship, cannot be the basis of my justification. Clearly, in Paul, it is not a relationship as an entity, the relational bond in itself, but a person that justifies and saves, specifically the person of "the Son of God, who loved me and gave himself for me" (Gal. 2:20). I suspect that position (2) above will inevitably gravitate to (3) in some form.

But, without developing a full discussion here, neither does Paul teach that justification is based on the ongoing renewing work of the Spirit in the believer. That is most apparent from the consideration that justification, as the nonimputation of sin, is the forgiveness of sin, the free remission of all sin—past, present, and future. Clearly, it is Christ's sacrifice for me, not the Spirit's work in me, that is the basis of my being forgiven. Certainly that renovating work is involved, especially in producing faith, but it is not the ground. How, as Paul views things, is it even conceivable that present, ongoing renewal could secure remission for past sin? To ask that question is to be at the answer: it cannot.

So we are left with the first of the three options just mentioned as the only viable one for Paul. In union with Christ, his righteousness is the ground of my being justified. That is, in my justification, his righteousness becomes my righteousness. But this, with the exclusion of the other two possibilities just noted, is virtually and necessarily to be at the notion of imputation. His righteousness is reckoned as mine. An imputative aspect is integral and indispensable to the justification given in union with Christ.

Calvin is worth quoting in this regard. In the course of his extensive discussion of justification in Book 3 of the *Institutes*, he concludes, "This is a wonderful plan of justification that . . . they [believers] should be accounted righteous outside themselves."[29] But a little earlier, before coming to this summary conclusion, he expresses how he understands, and does not understand, Christ being "outside" believers:

> Therefore, that joining together of Head and members, that indwelling of Christ in our hearts—in short, that *mystical union*—are accorded by us the highest degree of importance, so that Christ, having been made ours, makes us sharers with him in the gifts with which he has been endowed. We *do not, therefore, contemplate him outside ourselves from afar in order that his righteousness may be imputed to us but because we put on Christ and are engrafted into his body—in short, because he deigns to make us one with him.* For this reason, we glory that we *have fellowship of righteousness* with him.[30]

I am not sure how it could be said much better than that. Here we have someone who may not have thought in terms of a distinct theology of Paul, but who has well understood the mind—and heart—of the apostle.

29. Ibid., 1:740–41 (3.11.11).
30. Ibid., 1:737 (3.11.10) (italics added).

The Order of Salvation
and Eschatology—1

IN THE PREVIOUS CHAPTER, the personal appropriation of salvation in Paul was explored by tethering much of our discussion to the "center" of his gospel theology. As we saw, that center, focused as it is on Christ's death and resurrection, on messianic suffering and consequent glory, is eschatological to its core. Accordingly, being united to the crucified and resurrected Christ by faith—the essence of Paul's *ordo salutis*—is itself a thoroughly eschatological reality. In this and the following chapter, that eschatological factor is our controlling concern. Building on what we have already seen, how does Paul elaborate the eschatological salvation in Christ that is received by faith? What are the primary eschatological dimensions and soteriological implications of being united to Christ by faith? In addressing these questions, my interest in these chapters, as in the rest of the book, is in sketching the overall picture Paul provides and in making clear its basic dimensions. Many aspects of that picture, I recognize, are capable of being explored in much greater depth than I will be doing here.

Eschatology and Anthropology

We begin with, and will relate much of the discussion in this chapter to, 2 Corinthians 4:16, "Therefore we do not despair.

Though our outer man is decaying, yet our inner man is being renewed day by day." We take this verse as our further entrée into Paul because here, expressed in a nutshell, uniquely and more pointedly than anywhere else, is his anthropology of the Christian—how he views the constitution of the Christian's person as a Christian, how in that respect Christians are to look at themselves as Christians. Here we have Paul's basic outlook on the person of the Christian living between the resurrection and the return of Christ—on how, in fundamental categories, believers are to view themselves during this interim. In other words, this is a key text for issues related to salvation in its actual appropriation, for Paul's *ordo salutis*.

Several clarifying comments are in order as to its sense. First, Paul makes a categorical distinction. He sees the person of the Christian existing as both "inner man" and "outer man," a distinction present by implication in references to "the inner man" in Romans 7:22 and Ephesians 3:16. Despite the present trend in English usage to avoid the gender-neutral, generic masculine singular, for the sake of clarity in the discussion that follows, I will retain the traditional rendering (or "self") for the Greek word used here (*anthrōpos*) and reserve the alternative "person" to refer to the single subject of verse 16 who exists as both "outer" and "inner man."[1]

This distinction is not partitive, in terms of two distinct personal entities or natures. Paul is not saying that the Christian is a dual personality, a sort of schizophrenic or hybrid consisting of two persons, though, as we will presently note, there are partitive implications. The distinction, rather, is best taken as aspectual. It describes two ways of viewing the person of the

1. Among recent translations, alternatives for "man" are "nature" (ESV, NRSV), "human nature" (NJB), the adverbial contrast "outwardly"/"inwardly" (NIV, TNIV), and "bodies"/ "spirits" (NLT). These I judge for various reasons to be less adequate or inadequate. "Self" (NAB) seems to be the preferable alternative here.

Christian *as a whole*. In this regard, it is extremely important to keep in mind throughout the course of our discussion that it is the one "I," existing as both inner man and outer man, who is the *single*, total subject that does not "grow tired," become "discouraged" (NAB), or "give up" (NLT).[2] That is *not* said of the inner as distinct from the outer.

Elsewhere in Paul, on the one hand, "the outer man" is virtually equivalent to, or interchangeable with, "body" and "members," while "the inner man" is in view frequently in his use of "heart" or sometimes "spirit," understood as the human spirit.[3] As more careful examination beyond what I undertake here would show, the outer man or body is more than the narrowly physical or biotic. It is, as we might put it, the psycho-physical "package" that I am. It is I as a functioning person—as thinking, willing, speaking, and acting. All told, we may say, the outer self is the functioning I.

In distinction, "the inner self" or "heart" has in view who I am at the core of my being, in my *pre-functional* disposition. It is that disposition, more basic than my functioning, giving rise to my functioning and decisively controlling and finding expression in that functioning. As Paul views human beings in general and believers particularly, we are more than what we think or say or do.

It is fair to say that in verse 16, Paul expresses a certain definite, in fact quite fundamental, "split" in the person of the Christian. But he is not bifurcating or dichotomizing the Christian's personal makeup between an essential inner core and a disposable outer shell or covering. Rather, what is now true of the Christian as inner self is not (yet) true *for* the outer self. However, for

2. The translation "not lose heart" (NIV, ESV, NASB, NKJV) is surely defensible but less preferable in view of Paul's own usage; elsewhere "heart" (*kardia*) is close to or even identical with "the inner man."

3. See esp. H. Ridderbos, *Paul: An Outline of His Theology* (trans. J. R. de Witt; Grand Rapids: Eerdmans, 1975), 115–21.

the present, that is, until Christ returns, that is true only *within* the outer self. It is true only in the outer self for which the inner self is inner. Again, on balance, what is true for believers is not yet true *for* their bodies, but for now, until death (cf. 2 Cor. 5:8; Phil. 1:23) and looking toward the future resurrection of the body, it is true only *in* the body.

Within the immediately preceding context, what correlates most closely with verse 16, without being precisely identical, is verse 7, "We have this treasure in clay jars." This statement, which is, strictly speaking, autobiographical, surely includes a representative dimension that points to what is true for all believers. "This treasure" may be construed variously from the immediately preceding verses (vv. 4–6). It is either the gospel or its content: the eschatological glory of God in Christ or the person of Christ himself, the exalted Christ indwelling the believer. "Clay jars," in distinction, has in view the outer man of believers, believers in their bodily existence.

Second, to clear away a persisting misunderstanding, the distinction in 2 Corinthians 4:16 is not the same as the old man–new man distinction found elsewhere in Paul. He is clear that "our old man was crucified with Christ" (Rom. 6:6). In "putting on Christ" (Gal. 3:28), that is, in being united with Christ by faith, the Christian has "put off the old man and put on the new man" (Col. 3:9–10). The single subject in 2 Corinthians 4:16, the person as a whole who "does not despair," is the new man in Christ, the Christian existing, as noted, in the modes of both the inner and the outer man.

Third, "inner" and "outer" refer to opposite, in fact antithetical, principles operative in the Christian, realities as antithetical in their outcomes as death and life. "The outer self" is the subject, the I that I am, undergoing decay resulting in death. "The inner self" is the subject, the I that I am, marked by life—in fact, as we will see, eschatological life—and ongoing ("day by day") renewal.

With these clarifying comments on the sense of the passage, we may go on to relate the inner-outer distinction to what we have seen to be the heart of Paul's *ordo salutis*: union with the exalted Christ by faith. This union, given its obvious centrality, provides an important perspective on that distinction. At the same time, as we will see, the distinction qualifies how that union is presently realized.

In explicit anthropological terms or basic anthropological profile, 2 Corinthians 4:16 brings into view the impact or out-working of union with Christ in the life of the Christian. It shows that union as it is realized throughout the period between Christ's resurrection and his return. It spells out the basic situation, anthropologically, of that union during this period, in terms of both its present eschatological reality and the present limits on that reality.

Specifically, 2 Corinthians 4:16 reflects the basic "now and not yet" structure that qualifies our union with Christ and our sharing in its attendant benefits. In view here is our participation in the eschatological salvation revealed in Christ, as both realized and unrealized, as already present and still future. In view is the situation of the believer at any point between Christ's first and second comings. Expressed in terms of Paul's formal, overarching eschatological structure, this age (the pre- or non-eschatological order) and the age to come (the consummate, eschatological order) overlap throughout this period. Here we have captured, more clearly and categorically than elsewhere in Paul, as far as I can see, present participation in that eschatological salvation in a way that differentiates that participation specifically in terms of fundamental anthropological distinctions.

An important facet of verse 16, though often overlooked, is that its basic anthropological differentiation is drawn in a way that keeps the proverbial "already and not yet" from being distorted into an undifferentiated, yes-and-no dialectic, a matter we will address further below. Here we may note that it points to a clear yes for the inner self and a clear no for the outer self. The benefits of union with Christ are such, it appears, that insofar as I am outer self, that is, in terms of my bodily existence, those benefits are not yet possessed. My sharing in them is still future. On the other hand, as I am inner self or heart, considered for who I am at the core of my being, in my most basic bent or disposition, those benefits are already received and possessed; they are a present reality.

This fundamental state of affairs is given some clarification in the immediately following section (5:1–10). There Paul addresses the believer's hope of bodily resurrection, in other words, hope for the outer man. In this context, verse 7 affirms, "For we walk by faith, not by sight." This statement, proverbial in its ring, is an assertion like 4:16. It opens a fundamental perspective on the Christian life. Particularly instructive here is the way it serves to interpret 4:16 (as well as 4:7). "By faith" correlates with "the inner self" ("this treasure") and what is presently true for believers; "by sight" correlates with "the outer self" ("clay jars") and what is still future. For the present, until Jesus comes, our union with him and our sharing in the benefits of that union are "by faith," but not (yet) "by sight." We have our salvation for the present, all told, in the mode of believing, but as that believing falls short of seeing. Such "sight" participation in the benefits of union with Christ is reserved for what will be openly manifest in the resurrection of the body at his return (the predominating concern of the immediate context).

How, according to Paul, should we elaborate what we could dub his "soteriological anthropology," captured in its basic dimensions in 2 Corinthians 4:16? What for him are its primary ramifications? Here we will explore the answer to that question by bringing together distinctions already noted in the previous, as well as this, chapter and by focusing on their interplay or "mix": the distinctions between forensic and transforming, inner and outer, faith and sight, present and future. We will do that by taking as our basic reference point the distinction between the forensic and the renovative. We do so because that distinction specifies the fundamental, twofold benefits of union with Christ that redress the basic, twofold consequences of sin, its guilt and alienation as well as its corruption and enslavement. I begin, within the matrix defined by the distinctions just above, with a closer look at the renovative or transformative—in other words, at Paul's teaching on sanctification.

Eschatology and Sanctification

Union with Christ and the Resurrection

What bears highlighting about Paul's doctrine of sanctification and renewal can be seen in the way he views Christ's resurrection—in particular, how he relates it to the resurrection of Christians. Consistently, without exception, he stresses the unity that there is between Christ's resurrection and theirs, the solidarity that exists between him and them in being raised. The description of Christ in his resurrection as "the firstfruits of those who have fallen asleep" (1 Cor. 15:20) provides a point of departure into this strand of his teaching. Nowhere else in Paul is the unity or solidarity in resurrection presented so clearly and graphically.

The Future Bodily Resurrection of Christians. Specifically noteworthy in this verse is the use of "firstfruits" (*aparchē*). Johannes Weiss, in an early twentieth-century commentary on this passage, observed, "This little word contains a thesis." While we might well want to take exception to the linguistics reflected in this statement, in fact implicit in the use of the word here, in context, is the thought that not only underlies the entire argument in this epochal chapter 15 but much of Paul's teaching on the resurrection as a whole.

"Firstfruits" is an agricultural term, and its use here can be seen against the background of its Old Testament usage, where it has cultic significance, referring to certain sacrifices brought each year at the beginning of the spring harvest (Ex. 23:19; Lev. 23:10–11). That usage brings into view the initial portion of the harvest, the first installment of the whole. In doing so, however, it is not merely an indication of temporal priority. The notion of an organic connection or unity is also present and plainly essential. The firstfruits are the initial quantity brought into view only as they are a part of the whole, inseparable from the whole, and so in that sense represent the entire harvest.

In other words, Paul is saying here, the resurrection of Christ and of believers cannot be separated. Why? Because, to extend the metaphor as Paul surely intends, Christ's resurrection is the "firstfruits" of the resurrection "harvest" that includes the resurrection of believers. This thought is reinforced in verse 23: "Each in his own order: Christ the firstfruits, then at his coming those who belong to Christ."

For the sake of clarity, we should note that the resurrection of unbelievers is not in Paul's purview here (also true in 1 Thess. 4:14–18). In verse 20 and the rest of 1 Corinthians 15, the resurrection is seen in an entirely soteriological light. The solidarity in view is exclusively between Christ, as the firstfruits, and Christians; it does not include non-Christians. Paul, faithful to his Old Testament roots (e.g., Dan. 12:2), does recognize that the final resurrection will include unbelievers. That can be seen in his response to Felix in Acts 24:15, "There will be a resurrection of both the righteous and the wicked." But this aspect receives virtually no attention in his letters. Repeatedly and consistently, the resurrection is in view on its positive, saving side.

We must not miss the full impact of what Paul is saying here. For him it does not go far enough to say, as it is often put, that Christ's resurrection is the guarantee of our resurrection, in the sense of being certain because of God's eternal purpose or his word of promise to the church, although both are certainly true for Paul. Rather, Christ's resurrection is a guarantee in the sense that it is nothing less than the *actual* and, as such, representative beginning of the "general epochal event." In Paul's view, the general resurrection, as it includes believers, *begins* with Christ's resurrection.[4]

So we may fairly speculate, if Paul were present, say, at a modern-day prophecy conference and were asked, "When will the resurrection of believers take place?" the first thing he would likely say is, "It has already begun!" In Christ's resurrection, the end-time resurrection-harvest becomes a visible reality. This is one of the controlling thoughts that underlie his argument later in the chapter in verses 42–49.

Prominent, then, in Paul's description of the resurrected Christ as "the firstfruits" are two related considerations. The first is the eschatological significance of Christ's resurrection. His resurrection is not an isolated event in the past. Rather, in its undeniably full-bodied, past historicity, it belongs in a manner of speaking to the future. It can be said to be from the future and to have entered what is now the past and to be controlling the present from that future. In Christ's resurrection, as it may be variously put, the age to come has begun; the new creation has actually dawned; eschatological reality has been inaugurated.

Second is the primary point we have just been considering, the unity or solidarity that exists between the resurrection of Christ and the future resurrection of believers. We may say that for Paul these two resurrections are not so much two events, separate from each other, as they are two episodes, temporally distinct, of *one and the same* event. Together they form the beginning and end of the same "harvest."

---

4. G. Vos, *The Pauline Eschatology* (1930; Grand Rapids: Baker, 1979), 45 (on 1 Cor. 15:20, "Paul regards the resurrection of Jesus as the actual beginning of this general epochal event").

Much more briefly, we may note that in the immediately preceding paragraph, verses 12–19, this same notion of unity, anticipating and presupposing the ringing affirmation of verse 20, underlies and controls Paul's hypothetical, if-then argumentation. What is striking here is that Paul can argue in both directions: not only from Christ's resurrection to the resurrection of believers, but also back from their resurrection to Christ's. Negatively, a denial of the future resurrection of believers implies a denial of Christ's resurrection (vv. 13, 15, 16). The clear, controlling assumption is that the two resurrections are so intimately related that the one is given, inseparably, with the other. This way of arguing hypothetically in both directions points up the close bond and unity there is in Paul's thinking between the two. It confirms, as we have already put it, that the two resurrections are not so much separate occurrences as they are two episodes of the same event.

Elsewhere, among several other statements akin to 1 Corinthians 15:20, is the description of the exalted Christ as "firstborn from the dead" (Col. 1:18). Here "firstborn" (*prōtotokos*), unlike "firstfruits," does not of itself connote solidarity. Nor is it likely that his resurrection is being compared to the process of birth. Rather, against the background of its ample Old Testament usage (e.g., Ex. 4:22; Ps. 89:27 [Greek, 88:28]), "firstborn" signals his uniqueness and supremacy as resurrected. However, the qualifying prepositional phrase, "from the dead," brings solidarity into view. Just as he, by his resurrection, is out of or from among the dead (believers who will be raised), he is the "firstborn." "Firstborn from the dead," then, expresses his pre-eminence as already resurrected in solidarity with dead believers who are yet to be resurrected.

Already Raised with Christ. The passages looked at so far express the bond or unity there is between Christ's resurrection and the *future, bodily* resurrection of believers. In order to get the full picture of Paul's resurrection theology, however, we need to take note of other statements, where he speaks of the believer's resurrection using a verb in a past (Greek aorist or perfect) tense, and says that believers have already been raised with Christ (Eph. 2:5–6; Col. 2:12–13; 3:1; cf. Rom. 6:4–5, 8, 11, 13 and Gal. 2:20). How are we to understand such statements that affirm the resurrection as past for the Christian?

There is surely an important element of truth in holding that the past reference in the verses cited in the preceding paragraph has in view the involvement or solidarity of Christians with Christ at the time of his resurrection. In this sense, their resurrection was contemplated in his as he, their representative, was raised "for" them. Careful reading of these passages, however, reveals another aspect that is crucial and, in fact, primary. In view principally is what has taken place in the actual life history of the Christian, an involvement in this sense that is "existential."

There are several grounds for this understanding. First, in Ephesians 2:1–10, a key word is "walking," in the sense of a way of life and one's actual conduct. That idea brackets the passage. It opens with the readers' former, old-age, pre-Christian "walk" in the deadness of trespasses and sins (vv. 1, 5) and closes with their present "walk," instanced in the good works for which they have been created in Christ (v. 10). That contrast prompts a question. What explains this radical reversal in conduct, this 180-degree turnabout in "walk"? The answer is at the virtual midpoint of the passage—as we might say, its pivot point—in verses 5–6. What has effected this decisive change in conduct is having been made alive and having been raised with Christ.

An existential sense is also indicated in Colossians 2:12, where the resurrection with Christ in view takes place "through faith." Further, in Colossians 3:1–4, as well as in Romans 6:2–7:6, the resurrection contemplated is not only the motive, but also the basis, that provides the dynamic for actual obedience and holy living. So it is best understood as underlying and effecting personal transformation. Finally, in Romans 6 and Colossians 2, having been raised with Christ is among the benefits sealed to a person in baptism. For these reasons, then, having already been raised with Christ is real, actual, "existential," not something true merely "in principle" (whatever might be meant by that). The primary reference in the passages noted is to the ongoing application of salvation, not its once-for-all accomplishment. We may say that while the language used is that of the *historia salutis*, the reality described belongs to the *ordo salutis*. That way of putting it highlights the inseparability of *historia* and *ordo*, by virtue of union with Christ.

To sum up our observations so far, three factors shape Paul's teaching on the unity between Christ and believers in resurrection: (1) Christ's own resurrection, three days after his crucifixion; (2) the resurrection that occurs at the inception of life in Christ, the believer's initial appropriation of that salvation; and (3) future, bodily resurrection at Christ's return.

Furthermore, keeping in mind the organic connection between these three elements, that together they form a single "harvest," the basic pattern of Paul's teaching on resurrection may be expressed by saying that the unity of the resurrection of Christ and of Christians is such that the latter consists of two episodes in the experience of the individual believer: one that is past, already realized, and one that is still future, yet to be realized. Note how the formal structure of Paul's eschatology as a whole—the overlap of the two aeons, or world-ages, of the pre-eschatological and eschatological orders—is reflected in his teaching about what personally for believers is the fundamental eschatological occurrence; their resurrection is both already realized and still future.

Terminology. If we raise the question of terms to be used for distinguishing these two aspects, past and future, of the believer's resurrection, various more or less adequate proposals could be and have been made: "nonbodily-bodily," "internal-external," "invisible-visible," "secret-open." Decidedly unacceptable is "spiritual-physical" or "spiritual-bodily," at least if the adjective "spiritual" (*pneumatikos*) is used, as it should be, in its Pauline sense of referring (with the irrelevant exception of Ephesians 6:12) to the role and activity of the Holy Spirit.

When used in that sense, "spiritual" is no longer sufficient to discriminate between the two aspects of resurrection. The present, already realized resurrection is undoubtedly the work of the Spirit and so in that sense is properly labeled "spiritual." The problem, however, is that the bodily resurrection is no less "spiritual"—indeed is even more so. In the future resurrection of the body, the work of the Holy Spirit in the believer will reach its culmination, its ultimate realization, so that in 1 Corinthians 15:44 the single term of choice to describe the resurrection body is "spiritual," indicating that the body will be renovated and transformed by the Holy Spirit.

It is worth noting here in passing, to address a widespread, persisting misconception, that Paul's description of the resurrection body as "spiritual" does not describe its makeup, as if he intends to say that it is a body composed of an immaterial and in that sense "spiritual" substance and so is nonphysical. Quite to the contrary, he intends to affirm, in context (vv. 42–49), the transmuted but genuinely physical character of the believer's resurrection body, the eschatologically transformed physicality of the believer's person, as effected by the Holy Spirit in the resurrection. So with an eye to this spiritual transformation, the "spiritual" resurrected body is aptly labeled "transphysical."[5]

If we could ask Paul to provide labels for distinguishing the two aspects of resurrection, he would likely point us to our key

5. The term coined by N. T. Wright in *The Resurrection of the Son of God* (Christian Origins and the Question of God, vol. 3; London: SPCK, 2003), 477 ("the 'trans' is intended as a shortening of 'transformed.'"); see also 606–7, 612, 661.

verse, 2 Corinthians 4:16, and the distinction he makes there: as far as the believer is "inner man" ("heart," at the motivating center of his person), he is already raised; so far as the believer is "outer man" ("body," "members"), he is yet to be raised.

Some Related Observations. Paul's uniform—in fact, so far as I can see, invariable—accent on the unity between Christ and believers in resurrection, is reinforced in an indirect but pervasive way by numerous statements that simply refer to the fact of Christ's resurrection without any amplification. There are two kinds of such statements (in almost all of which the verb is a form of *egeirō*). In one, the verb is active, with God (more specifically, the Father) as the subject and Jesus (variously designated) as the direct object (e.g., Rom. 10:9; Gal. 1:1). Alternatively, the verb is passive with Jesus as its subject (e.g., Rom. 4:25; 1 Cor. 15:20).

When these undeveloped references to the resurrection are surveyed as a group, a consistent and unmistakable pattern emerges. God, in his specific identity as the Father, raises Jesus; correlatively, Jesus is passive in his resurrection. This viewpoint is maintained consistently by Paul, without exception as far as I can see. Nowhere does he say that Christ was active in his resurrection, much less that he raised himself. Paul does not teach that Christ "rose" from the dead, but that he "was raised." In 1 Thessalonians 4:14, "Jesus died and rose again" is only an apparent exception, as is shown by the parallel statement in verse 16, "the dead in Christ will rise first." Here Paul no more intends to say that Christ was active in his resurrection than that Christians, in union with Christ, will be active in theirs.[6] The stress everywhere is on the enlivening power and activity of the Father, of which Christ is the recipient and beneficiary.

The theological significance of this stress plainly lies in what we have seen to be the controlling unity that there is between

6. The intransitive verb forms in each instance (*anestē*, v. 14; *anastēsontai*, v. 16) describe action without indicating active agency.

the resurrection of Christ and the resurrection of believers. Christ's passivity in his resurrection reflects his identification and solidarity with believers in being raised from the dead. For Paul—certainly not in conflict with, but other than, the way it is often understood—the resurrection is not the especially evident display and powerful proof of Christ's divinity, but rather the vindication of the incarnate Christ in his suffering and obedience unto death, and with that vindication, the powerful transformation of him in his humanity. In the terms of Romans 1:4, by virtue of the resurrection he is now, comparatively, what he was not previously, "the Son of God in power."[7]

At the same time, on balance, in this solidarity only Christ is the "firstfruits" and the "firstborn." He alone is the last Adam with all, as noted earlier, that attaches to that unique identity. Specifically, and having a particular bearing on sanctification, in 1 Corinthians 15:42–45, while in his resurrection he is the first exemplification of the "spiritual body" that believers will also have, he and he alone is the "life-giving Spirit." That is, as noted earlier in discussing union with Christ, in his resurrection he has been so thoroughly transformed by the Holy Spirit and has come into such complete and final possession of the Spirit, that consequently they are one in the work of giving resurrection life, of bestowing eschatological life. The presence of the Holy Spirit in the church and as he indwells all believers is the indwelling presence of the exalted Christ in his resurrection life and power, as Romans 8:9–11, as noted earlier, especially shows.

Some comment should be made here on the relationship of Paul's invariable emphasis on the passivity of Jesus in his resurrection to Jesus' own statements elsewhere suggesting

---

7. Or, "the powerful Son of God," taking the prepositional phrase "in power" adjectivally rather than adverbially. On the relative comparison effected by the resurrection, cf. esp. 2 Cor. 13:4, "He was crucified in weakness, but lives [now, in contrast] by the power of God."

or affirming that he actively rose from the dead.[8] With an eye
to the issue of the overall unity of New Testament theology,
these viewpoints are not in conflict, but complementary. Later
church reflections stemming from the formulation of the
Council of Chalcedon (451) concerning the mystery of Christ's
two-natured person are helpful at this point. Among those
reflections, anything true of either of Christ's natures, in
distinction from the other, is true of him as a person. Accordingly, Paul looks at the resurrection in terms of the Adamic
identity of Jesus and the genuine humanity he shares with
believers, while Jesus in John's gospel affirms what is also true
because of the deity he shares with the Father in his unique
identity and relationship as the Son.

   Conclusion. Two considerations may be underlined from
these reflections on the basic structure of Paul's theology of the
resurrection. First, it is not an overstatement to say, as Paul sees
things, that at the core of their being, in the deepest recesses
of who they are—in other words, in "the inner self"—believers
will never be more resurrected than they already are. God has
done a work in each believer, a work of nothing less than resurrection proportions, that will not be undone. Such language,
it needs to be stressed, is not just a metaphor. When Paul says
that believers have already been raised with Christ, we are not
simply dealing with a loose, figurative adaptation of the language
of resurrection, with an evocative but not strictly literal way of
expressing present renewal.[9] In terms of Paul's anthropology,

8. E.g., most emphatically in John's gospel: "Destroy this temple, and in
three days I will raise it up" (2:19); "I lay down my life that I may take it up
again. No one takes it from me, but I lay it down of my own accord. I have
authority to lay it down, and I have authority to take it up again" (10:17–18).
   9. I cannot see that the view, e.g., of N. T. Wright, that the language of
passages like Eph. 2:5–6; Col. 3:1 is metaphorical (*Resurrection of the Son of
God*, 237–40, 478, 681), takes adequate account of the anthropology of 2 Cor.
4:16 and its implications.

the past resurrection of the inner man is to be understood as realistically and literally as future, bodily resurrection. Believers experience the ongoing renewal ("day by day") spoken of in 2 Corinthians 4:16, based on the resurrection of the inner man. In Philippians 1:6, where Paul assures the church that "the one who began a good work in you will bring it to completion at the day of Jesus Christ," that "good work" begun is rooted in nothing less than a work of resurrection.

By now, second, it should be apparent that in Paul there is no more important conclusion about the Christian life, nothing about its structure that is more basic than this consideration: the Christian life in its entirety is to be subsumed under the category of resurrection. Pointedly, the Christian life is resurrection life. In terms of the metaphor of 1 Corinthians 15:20, the Christian life is part of the resurrection-harvest inaugurated by Christ's own resurrection. The place of Christians, their share, in that harvest is now—not only in the future, but presently. The Christian life is a manifestation, an outworking, of the resurrection life and power of the resurrected Christ, become the "life-giving Spirit" (1 Cor. 15:45). It is in this light that statements like Galatians 2:20 ("I no longer live, but Christ lives in me")—autobiographical, but surely applicable to every Christian—ought to be read.

This sweeping conclusion about the Christian life obviously has wide-ranging implications and is capable of being amplified and developed along a number of lines. Here, to take up just one of them that is particularly instructive for our larger interest, I focus on Paul's *parenesis*, his exhortations and commands to the church. Or, viewed somewhat more broadly, our interest is in aspects of the ethics of Paul.

Indicative and Imperative

A good place to begin considering the hortatory element in Paul's theology is Colossians 3:1–4 and the way the resurrection life of believers is presented there. On the one hand, their resurrection is referred to as an already-accomplished fact: "You have been raised with Christ." Again, through their union with Christ, resurrection life is what believers already have and enjoy: "You have died and your life is hidden with Christ in God" (v. 3).

At the same time, however, interwoven with these statements are two parallel commands, "Seek the things above" (v. 1), and "Set your mind on the things above" (v. 2). Here "the things above"[10] surely refers to things that pertain to the life of the resurrected and ascended Christ. That is clear from the relative clause in verse 1; "above" is specifically "where Christ is sitting at the right hand of God." In other words, resurrection (or ascension) life is now a matter of aspiration—something, in some sense, still to be attained.

This "above," it should be appreciated, is not timeless or ahistorical in the sense of being beyond time or having its validity apart from history. It is not the "above" of a metaphysical dualism. Rather, we may say, it is a redemptive-historical "above." In view is heaven as the place it now is, because for now, until his return, the exalted Christ is present there. In these verses, then, resurrection life is brought into view as both a possession and a goal; it is both a gift and a task. The controlling thought here may be paraphrased in the somewhat paradoxically sounding directive, "Seek after, set your mind on what you already have."

This teaching is capable of being stated in different ways, but instructive here is the way it shapes or is reflected in the syntax of verse 1—in its composition, a conditional clause and a main clause or consequent. In the conditional clause, "if you have been raised with Christ," the verb is in the indicative mood. In the consequent, the main clause, "seek the things above," the verb is an imperative. So Paul is saying, "If the indicative, then the imperative," or concretely, "If you have resurrection life, then seek resurrection life." Or, assuming as we should from the context,

10. In the Greek text (*ta anō*), the adverb translated "above" is used as a noun and made definite in the plural.

immediate and broader, that this condition is realized,[11] "Because you have resurrection life, seek resurrection life." Or yet again, transposing the grammatical structure, "Seek after what you already have, because you already have it."

In the study of Paul in the modern period, this pattern of teaching has been the object of a fair amount of discussion and is often referred to as "the problem of indicative and imperative in Paul." While this teaching certainly challenges the church, it is not ultimately problematic and might better be referred to as the "pattern" or "phenomenon" of indicative and imperative in Paul. In addition to Colossians 3:1–4, the following passages display this pattern:

Galatians 5:25: "If we live in the Spirit, let us walk in the Spirit"—virtually equivalent to "If we live in the Spirit, let us live in the Spirit."

Galatians 5:1: "Christ has set us free for freedom; stand firm and don't be burdened again with a yoke of slavery"—equivalent in its elemental thrust to "You are free; therefore, be free."

Ephesians 5:8: "But now you are light in the Lord; walk as children of light."

1 Corinthians 5:7: "Get rid of the old leaven that you may become a new batch of dough [= "become unleavened"], even as you are unleavened."

Galatians 3:27 (the indicative): "You have put on Christ"; Romans 13:14 (the imperative, addressed to the church): "Put on the Lord Jesus Christ."

Colossians 3:9–10 (the indicative): Believers "have put off the old man and put on the new"; Ephesians 4:22–24 (the imperative,

11. So, e.g., the NIV: "Since, then, you have been raised with Christ . . ."

on the most likely reading): They are to "put off the old and put on the new."

Romans 6:2 (the indicative): "You have died to sin"; verse 12 (the imperative): "Do not let sin reign in your mortal body."

More broadly, sanctification and renewal are seen, on the one hand, as the gift and work of God (1 Cor. 1:2; Phil. 1:6; 1 Thess. 5:23) and, on the other hand, as engaging the believer's activity (2 Cor. 7:1; cf. outside Paul, Heb. 12:14). Similarly, what in Galatians 5:22 is "the fruit of the Spirit" is in Romans 6:22 "your fruit." Again, love, the first of the fruit of the Spirit (Gal. 5:22), is also the first commandment (Rom. 13:8–9).

Such statements, taken together, have prompted the observation that Paul's exhortations to the church as a whole, his ethics of the Christian life in their entirety, can be summed up in the epigram, "Become what you are." This is helpful, but by itself it carries a liability that can render it decidedly unhelpful (suggesting some form of personal autonomy), unless it is read with an all-encompassing Christological gloss, "Become what you are *in Christ.*"

If we go on now to ask about the relationship between indicative and imperative, we pose a question that in fact takes us to the heart of Paul's understanding of the Christian life as a whole. It shows, too, although we cannot explore it here, how thoroughly he is a covenantal theologian. Negatively, to misconstrue that relationship strikes at the core of his teaching on sanctification. In addressing that relational question, I do so on the assumption, with an eye to discussions that we are unable to address here, that they belong together in a positive, nonpolar, nondialectical relationship. That is, the presence of both indicative and imperative in Paul's teaching does not amount to a contradiction, whether outright or apparent, to be dealt with by interpretive strategies that have the effect of eliminating or nullifying one or the other. The indicative is not a disguised imperative, nor is the imperative a hidden indicative.

Further, since the terms *indicative* and *imperative* are by themselves abstract, it is worth reminding ourselves briefly here that, concretely, the indicative is the salvation accomplished once-for-all in Christ and received in being united to him by faith, while the imperative has in view the law of God, with the Ten Commandments at its core. That the latter is the case can be seen from 1 Corinthians 7:19, "For neither circumcision counts for anything nor uncircumcision, but keeping the commandments of God" (ESV). Here "the commandments of God," in the light of Romans 7:12 ("the law is holy, and the commandment is holy, righteous and good"), Romans 13:8–10, and Ephesians 6:2–3, are best understood as the Decalogue, centered in the love command. Unpersuasive, in my judgment, are arguments that the phrase "the commandments of God" in 1 Corinthians 7:19 does not refer to any of the Ten Commandments directly, but only insofar as they may be found among the imperatives present in either the teaching of Jesus or of Paul or both.

There are two important and related points to be made about the indicative-imperative relationship. First, that relationship is *irreversible*. The indicative has priority in the sense that it is the foundation that grounds the imperative. The imperative is the fruit of the indicative, not the reverse. If it needs saying, Paul's gospel, as gospel, stands or falls with this irreversibility. To put it negatively, it is not as if the indicative is constituted by the imperative or expresses only a possibility that is first actualized by the imperative (e.g., Bultmann). Rather, the indicative provides the impulse or incentive toward fulfilling the imperative.

Paul, we may observe, never writes in the imperative without first writing, at least implicitly, in the indicative. That is so because he knows all too well, better than some subsequent preachers, that "it does no good to beat a dead horse"—exactly what the congregation is apart from Christ, apart from who they are and what they have in him.

But this irreversible relationship is at the same time an *insepara-rable* relationship. Paul, we may also generalize, never writes in the indicative without having the imperative in view, at least implicitly. On balance, the imperative without the indicative leads into soteriological legalism, to using the imperative either to achieve or to secure one's salvation; it leaves us with Paul the moralist. On the other hand, the indicative without the imperative tends to antinomianism; it leaves us with Paul the mystic.

The point to be grasped here is that the indicative does not describe a reality that exists by itself, one to which a heart for the imperative or a positive response to it follows as a subsequent, presumably detachable addition. Rather, indicative and impera-tive are given together, and compliance with the imperative is the consequence and attestation apart from which the indicative does not exist. Paul's exhortations are a clear indication that the life of new obedience does not result automatically in those united to Christ and justified by faith.

The imperative has a critical or discriminating function. Where the indicative is present, a reality, there concern for the imperative must and will be a reality that comes to expression, however imperfectly, minimally, or inadequately. Herman Rid-derbos has a helpful way of putting the matters at issue here, striking the requisite balance. For Paul the imperative, no less than the indicative, is the concern of *faith*. Both indicative and imperative are the object of faith, as faith in Christ, and they are that together and inseparably. On the one hand, faith in its *receptivity* answers to the indicative, while on the other hand, faith in its *activity* answers to the imperative.[12]

12. Ridderbos, *Paul*, 256. I would be remiss not to note here, among a con-siderable amount of literature on the indicative and the imperative and their relationship, the substantial influence that his discussion as a whole (pp. 253–58) has had on my comments.

Perhaps the deepest perspective in Paul on the indicative-imperative relationship is provided in Philippians 2:12–13: "Therefore, my dear friends, as you have always obeyed—not only in my presence, but now much more in my absence—continue to work out your salvation with fear and trembling, for it is God who works in you to will and to act according to his good purpose" (NIV). Here the imperative, sweeping in its scope, comes first: you, the church, are to continue working out your salvation with fear and trembling, fully devoted and engaged. Then, equally sweeping, the indicative follows: God is at work in you, both to will and to work what pleases him.

Noteworthy is the way Paul conjoins the two here. Negatively, he does not say that the indicative of God's working parallels our working. Nor does he say that God's activity supplements ours, or ours his. Nor is there even the suggestion of a tension, as if God is at work in spite of us or to compensate for the defects in our doing. Rather, we are working just *because* (*gar*, "for") God is working.

Here is what may be fairly called a synergy, but it is not that of a divine-human partnership, in the sense of a cooperative enterprise with each side making its own contribution. It is not a 50/50 undertaking (nor even 99.44 percent God and 0.56 percent ourselves[13]). Involved here is, as it could be put, the "mysterious math" of God's covenant, of the relationship, restored in Christ, between the Creator and his image-bearing creature, whereby 100% + 100% = 100%. Sanctification is 100 percent the work of God and, just for that reason, it is to engage 100 percent of the activity of the believer.

These reflections on indicative and imperative may be integrated into the larger present-future eschatological structure of Paul's *ordo salutis*. That can be done by taking a cue from Romans 6:12–13:

13. The allusion is to a soap commercial from a bygone era, which some older readers may remember!

Therefore do not let sin reign in your mortal body, to obey its lusts. And do not present your members as instruments of unrighteousness to sin, but present yourselves to God as alive from the dead, and your members as instruments of righteousness to God.

Here Paul draws together important threads of his discussion to this point in Romans 6 in a way that at the same time advances his argument. A permissible transformation of the surface construction reads, "If you are alive from the dead, present yourselves in your mortal bodies for righteousness, not unrighteousness." That phrasing points up its similarity to Colossians 3:1 and other passages noted in considering the indicative-imperative pattern.

In particular, we may highlight two phrases in these verses, "alive from the dead" (v. 13) and "in [the] mortal body" (v. 12). Correlating them serves to bring out how Paul views the Christian life as a whole. In fact, nothing better brings to a focus the structure and true "dialectic" of the present existence of the believer than this correlation: "alive from the dead . . . in the mortal body." Nothing in Paul, it seems, provides a more basic perspective on that existence.

It is worth noting briefly how this structure can be put alternatively in the terms of other passages in Paul, some of which we have already noted. Believers are alive with the new-creation life of the age to come, as they continue to live in "the present evil age" (Gal. 6:14–15 with 1:4). Again, they are those who walk "not according to the flesh, but according to the Spirit in the flesh" (Rom. 8:4 with 2 Cor. 10:3). Or again, they are those who have "this treasure in clay jars" (2 Cor. 4:7), those who "walk by faith and not by sight" (2 Cor. 5:7).

Finally, reading the indicative-imperative pattern in the light of this structure, superimposing the one on the other, yields the following overall picture. "Alive from the dead" pinpoints the *present* indicative of eschatological salvation, salvation as *already* possessed in Christ, and so specifies the *basis* and *dynamic* for obeying the imperative. This is the first thing that the congregation, by faith, needs to know and be continually reminded about itself. On the other hand, "in [the] mortal body" pinpoints the *future* indicative of this salvation, salvation as not yet revealed and possessed in Christ, and so specifies the *need* for the imperative and its *scope*, the necessity that the congregation be exhorted.

Historical and Theological Reflections

The Reformation tradition has clearly grasped, as Paul teaches, the eschatological "not yet" of our sanctification, to be realized only penultimately at death and consummately at Christ's return. It has recognized that our being perfectly conformed to the image of Christ is still future and will not occur until his return and the resurrection of the body. It has maintained that truth more or less consistently, even though at times some have been drawn away, for example, toward various cheap perfectionisms and easy "victorious life" positions.

But, we may ask, has the Reformation tradition grasped as clearly the "resurrection," the eschatological "already," of our sanctification? For instance, as we consider preaching and teaching in our traditions, how many Christians understand that the Holy Spirit presently at work in them is nothing less than resurrection power, that the Spirit, through whom God "will give life to your mortal bodies," is "his Spirit who dwells in you" (Rom. 8:11)? How many believers grasp that the Holy Spirit indwelling them is an eschatological power—that the Spirit, in his activity in the church, is an actual "down payment" on our eschatological inheritance (2 Cor. 1:22; 5:5; Eph. 1:14), the "firstfruits" of the full "harvest" of his eschatological working (Rom. 8:23)? How many appreciate that Christ himself, as "life-giving Spirit" (1 Cor. 15:45), is present and at work in our lives in his resurrection power?

We rightly confess, with Lord's Day 44 of the Heidelberg Catechism (answer 114), that we, "in this life, have only a small beginning of this obedience." But do we appreciate that, from the vantage point of the apostle, that beginning is nothing less than eschatological at its core, that as the "good work begun in us," bound for completion at Christ's return (Phil. 1:6), it stems from a definitive and irreversible work that has nothing less than resurrection proportions?

In the matter of sanctification, it seems to me, we must confront a tendency—which is, unless my impression is wrong, pervasive within churches of the Reformation—to view the gospel and salvation in its outcome almost exclusively in terms of justification. Recall, for instance, the statement of a conference speaker quoted in the previous chapter to the effect that the gospel is only about what Christ has done "for us" and apparently does not include his work, through the Spirit, "in us."

The effect of this outlook, whether or not intended—and no doubt it is often the latter—is that sanctification tends to be seen as the response of the believer to salvation defined in terms of justification. Sanctification is viewed as an expression of gratitude from our side for our justification and the free forgiveness of our sins, usually with the accent on the imperfection and inadequacy of such expressions of gratitude. Sometimes there is even the suggestion that while sanctification is highly desirable and its lack is certainly unbecoming and inappropriate, it is not really necessary in the life of the believer, not really integral to our salvation and an essential part of what it means to be saved from sin. The attitude we may have—at least this is the way it comes across—is something like, "If Jesus did that for you, died that your sins might be forgiven and entitled you to heaven, shouldn't you at least do this for him, try to please him?"

With such a construction, justification and sanctification are pulled apart; the former is what God does, and the latter is what we do and do so inadequately. At worst, this outlook tends to devolve into a deadening moralism. What takes place, in effect, is the reintroduction of a refined or perhaps not so refined works-principle, more or less divorced from, and so in tension with, the faith that justifies. Self-affirming works, those self-securing and self-assuring efforts, so resolutely resisted and turned away at the front door of justification, return by creeping in through the back door of sanctification. The "faith" and "works" that God intends to be joined together in those he has restored to his fellowship and service (cf., e.g., Jas. 2:18), through uniting them to Christ by faith, are pulled apart and at best exist in an uneasy tension, a tension that can paralyze the Christian life and render obedience less than uninhibited and wholehearted.

I hope not to have caricatured anyone here. Readers will have to judge the accuracy of my perceptions and whether they square with their own impressions and experiences. I hope, too, not to be misunderstood here. Surely our gratitude is important. How could we be anything but grateful for the free forgiveness of our sins? That note of gratitude, whether or not explicit, is pervasive and unmistakable in Paul (e.g., Gal. 2:20; 1 Tim. 1:12–16). No doubt, too, all of our efforts as believers are, at best, imperfect and flawed by our continuing to sin. But Paul sounds a different, much more radical note about sanctification and the good works of Christians. Sanctification, first of all and ultimately, is not a matter of what we do, but of what God does. As the best in the Reformation tradition recognizes, it, no less than our justification, is a work of his grace.[14]

Further, there should be little difficulty now in recognizing, given his teaching on the already-realized aspect of the believer's resurrection, that for Paul sanctification is not only a process involving us in our activity, but also and first of all "definitive sanctification"—a decisive, definitive, once-for-all act of God, underlying our activity.[15] A central point of Romans 6–7, for

14. See, e.g., the answers in Westminster Larger Catechism 75 and Westminster Shorter Catechism 35.

15. This aspect of New Testament teaching on sanctification, primarily in Paul, warrants much greater attention than I am able to give it here. The expression "definitive sanctification" appears to have originated with John Murray. See his important discussion in *Collected Writings of John Murray* (4

instance, is that while sin is a continuing reality for the believer, it is not my lord. Because of union with Christ in his death and resurrection, I am no longer sin's slave. Sin is indwelling, but not overpowering; for the believer, indwelling sin is not enslaving sin.

In fact, as we have already seen, sanctification is an aspect and outcome of the reality of the resurrection already experienced by the believer, and the process of its realization has no deeper perspective from which it can be viewed than that it is a continual "living to God" by those who are "alive from the dead" (to be sure, "in the mortal body," Rom. 6:11–13). Or, as Paul puts it in Ephesians 2:10—there is no more decisive biblical pronouncement on "good works"—sanctification is a matter of those—note, just those who are "saved by grace through faith and not by works" (vv. 8–9)—who "have been created in Christ Jesus for good works, which God prepared beforehand that we should walk in them."

The point here is that "the path of good works runs not from man to God, says Paul, but from God to man."[16] Ultimately, in the deepest sense, for Paul "our good works" are not *ours*, but God's. They are his work, begun and continuing in us, his being "at work in us, both to will and to do what pleases him" (Phil. 2:13). That is why, without any tension, a faith that rests in God the Savior is a faith that is restless to do his will.

In 1 Corinthians 4:7, Paul puts to the church some searching rhetorical questions: "Who makes you different from anyone else? What do you have that you did not receive? And if you did receive it, why do you boast as though you did not?" (NIV). These questions, we should be sure, have the same answer for sanctification as for justification, for our good works as well as for

---

vols.; Edinburgh: Banner of Truth, 1976–82), 2:277–93; see also his *Principles of Conduct: Aspects of Biblical Ethics* (Grand Rapids: Eerdmans, 1957), 202–28 ("The Dynamic of the Biblical Ethics").

16. G. C. Berkouwer, *Faith and Sanctification* (trans. J. Vriend; Grand Rapids: Eerdmans, 1952), 191.

our faith. Both, faith and good works, are God's gift, his work in us. The deepest motive for our sanctification, for holy living and good works, is not our psychology, not how I "feel" about God and Jesus. Nor is it even our faith. Rather, that profoundest of motives is the resurrection power of Christ and the new creation that we are and have already been made a part of in Christ by his Spirit.

The Order of Salvation and Eschatology—2

Eschatology and Justification

From our reflections on sanctification and personal renewal in the previous chapter we turn again to the forensic or legal aspect of salvation in Paul, in particular to his teaching on justification. We do that now with this question in mind: how should we view that teaching in the light of the basic, already–not yet anthropological profile on union with Christ expressed in 2 Corinthians 4:16?

Initial Considerations

We begin with an all-important historical observation. The Reformation tradition, as previously noted, has not so clearly grasped the eschatological "already" of sanctification, the nothing less than resurrection dimensions of the renewal of the Christian. Quite in contrast, however, has been its discovery or recapture of the eschatological "already" of justification. This grasp is perhaps implicit, but it is definite and clear in effect, however often it has been compromised or not adequately appreciated. In fact, it is probably not an overstatement to say that this rediscovery was the most important soteriological contribution of the Reformation. Certainly none is more important.

For instance, in a verse like Romans 8:1, "There is therefore now no condemnation for those who are in Christ Jesus," Luther and others, implicitly if not explicitly, heard an eschatological pronouncement. They understood that the "now" (*nyn*) in this verse has definitive, settled, and final force; it is the "now" of eschatological realization.

In late medieval Roman Catholicism, the future verdict at the final judgment was the uncertain outcome of the Christian life. In contrast, the Reformers came to understand that, in effect, the verdict belonging at the end of history has been brought forward and already pronounced on believers in history, and so constitutes the certain and stable basis for the Christian life and provides unshakeable confidence in the face of the final judgment.

But now, what about justification and the "not yet" of our salvation? Should we, according to Paul, think of our justification as in some sense still future? In other words, should we see his teaching on justification in terms of his already–not yet outlook on salvation and within the inner-outer anthropological grid provided by 2 Corinthians 4:16?

An initial reaction might be that the answer is negative— and an emphatic no at that. The reason for this reaction is not only understandable, but bound to be appreciated. To speak of justification as in any sense "not yet" appears to take away from its "already," definitive character. To view it as in some sense still future seems to threaten its present, absolute finality, to undermine its settled certainty in the life of the Christian.

I wish, then, to be as clear as I can that it would certainly betray or misrepresent Paul if anything said in this regard here (or elsewhere, for that matter) would be heard or allowed to call into question that settled certainty. That is no more or less the case than it would be to question for him the settled certainty of the believer's already having been resurrected with Christ because the resurrection of the body is still future. In fact, as we will presently see, this observation has particular, inner relevance for justification.

At the outset, it should be noted that explicit references in Paul to justification as still future for believers, if present at all, are minimal. Among the passages usually cited are Romans 2:13, Romans 5:19, Galatians 5:5, and 2 Timothy 4:8, but all are contested. My own view is that at least some of these passages and perhaps others are plausibly, even most likely, to be read as referring to an actual future justification for believers or to a future aspect of their justification. However, I am not able here to enter into the kind of detailed exegesis that would be necessary to make treatment of them profitable, especially in view of the intensive attention that Romans 2:13 continues to receive. The discussion that follows, in taking the direction it does, does have a partial and at points somewhat provisional character. It is certainly capable of being amplified, and at places may have to be recast or corrected. But I offer it as providing in the main a stable basis for further reflection on the issue it addresses.

In fact, there is value in bracketing the passages noted in the preceding paragraph from our consideration in the interest of showing that the case for a future aspect to the Christian's justification or, put another way, for a decisive future aspect to the forensic side of salvation that is tantamount to justification, does not rest on such passages alone or even primarily. That case, as I will make it here, has four components: (1) a presumptive consideration stemming from the structure of Paul's soteriology and eschatology, (2) the forensic significance that both death, including bodily death, and resurrection have for him, (3) his teaching on adoption, and (4) his teaching on the final judgment.

The Perspective of the Westminster Standards

Before considering these four components, it will be useful to introduce into our discussion a perspective with confessional status in Reformation orthodoxy, that found in the Westminster

Standards. Westminster Larger Catechism 90 asks, "What shall be done to the righteous at the day of judgment?" In a similar vein is Shorter Catechism 38, "What benefits do believers receive from Christ at the resurrection?" In both instances the answer includes the affirmation that on the day of judgment believers, as they are said to be righteous, shall be "openly acknowledged and acquitted."[1]

The point, plain in both catechisms, is that Christians will be included in the final judgment. At the risk of belaboring the obvious, for them it will have forensic or legal significance. It will be relevant personally as judgment. They will in fact be judged at the final judgment. Specifically, for them the outcome contemplated, or we may also say the verdict to be rendered, will be their acquittal; they will be "openly acquitted." In other words, of any charges to the contrary conceivably contemplated, they will be declared not guilty, and that will happen publicly. It is not to be missed that in the Shorter Catechism this acquittal is among the "benefits" received from Christ. Also, it is said to be "open" or public, an important factor that will occupy us in detail below.

To be "acquitted" and to be "justified" are largely interchangeable terms. While, biblically considered, the two are not fully synonymous, they overlap in meaning; acquittal is at the heart of justification. So these catechisms teach, in effect, that for believers the final judgment, as it involves their being acquitted, will have justifying significance; in some sense it will be their justification, their being declared to be righteous.

We may conclude, then, by clear implication, that the notion of the believer's justification as in some sense future, or having a future aspect, has confessional grounding in Reformation orthodoxy. That notion does not stem from the historical-critical study of Paul in the modern era. Nor is it a recent discovery bound up with the New Perspective on Paul. It is not foreign to,

---

1. The supporting texts cited, in order, are Matt. 25:33 and 10:32 (Larger Catechism) and Matt. 25:23 and 10:32 (Shorter Catechism).

or in conflict with, the heritage of the Reformation, but rather is given with that heritage.[2]

Justification as Future

A Presumptive Consideration. But now, what about Paul? How does this confessional position square with his theology? We can begin addressing that question with what might be viewed as a presumptive consideration, bound up with the structure of his theology, or, more particularly, the basic pattern of his soteriology, already discussed in Chapter 2. To put the issue negatively, there is no place in Paul for a justification that (1) would fall outside of union with the exalted Christ by faith, that is, would not be a benefit given with that union,[3] (2) would not be qualified by the

2. I should perhaps narrow the scope of this concluding statement to Reformed orthodoxy, since I am unaware, though without extensive study, of similar statements in Lutheran confessions and theology.

Among Reformed writers who speak of justification as in some sense future are R. Dabney, *Systematic Theology* (1871; repr., Edinburgh: Banner of Truth, n.d.), 645; J. Fisher, *The Assembly's Shorter Catechism Explained, by Way of Question and Answer* (Glasgow: William Smith, 1779), 251–52; J. Flavel, *An Exposition of the Assembly's Shorter Catechism*, in *The Whole Works of the Reverend Mr. John Flavel* (Edinburgh: Andrew Anderson, 1701), 832; J. Owen, *The Doctrine of Justification by Faith* (1677; repr., *The Works of John Owen*, vol. 5; Edinburgh: Banner of Truth, 1965), 159–60; F. Turretin, *Institutes of Elenctic Theology* (1679; trans. G. M. Giger; Phillipsburg, NJ: P&R, 1994), 2:685 (16.9.11–12); H. Witsius, *The Economy of the Covenants between God and Man* (1677; trans. William Crookshank; Escondido, CA: Den Dulk Christian Foundation, 1990), 1:418–24 (book 3, ch. 8, para. 63–77). My thanks to Robert Tarullo and Peter Wallace for alerting me to some of these sources.

3. This, along with the other two factors that follow, is true of New Testament believers, not old covenant believers, who lived when Christ was not yet exalted. Paul is clear (e.g., Rom. 3–4; Gal. 3) that old and new covenant believers are both justified in the same way, by faith (the giving of the law at Sinai making no difference in that respect). Old covenant believers had their justification (and other benefits of salvation, including regeneration that created their faith) in communion with the Lord, but that bond of fellowship only anticipated the consummate form that bond now has: union with Christ as he has been and is exalted. In this regard, the *ordo salutis* (application of redemption) does differ for old and new covenant believers.

This qualification does not affect the already–not yet structure of justification being considered here. There is no good reason for questioning that, in

inner-outer anthropology of 2 Corinthians 4:16, and so (3) would fall outside of the already–not yet pattern of receiving salvation that qualifies that union. In other words, a future justification of the Christian at Christ's return, in the resurrection of the body and at the final judgment, as we will see, is a "good and necessary consequence," fully consonant with Paul's teaching.

Arguing the contrary would face a difficulty that is substantial, if not insuperable, in my judgment. One would have to show how isolating justification from the already–not yet structure of receiving salvation, in particular its "not yet" aspect, would be compatible with or coherent within Paul's soteriology centered on union with Christ and involving the inner-outer anthropology reflected in 2 Corinthians 4:16.

This observation, I recognize, may not be persuasive to everyone, at least at this point in our discussion. But it should carry weight with those who recognize that the Pauline corpus presents its readers with a structure of theological thinking and the corresponding need to wrestle with the full dimensions of that theology. Whatever the apparent liabilities, then, Paul's teaching on justification, we may fairly anticipate, has its place within and reflects the already–not yet pattern of his soteriology. But we are not left only with this presumption.

Death and Resurrection. As we saw in the previous chapter, union with Christ in his resurrection, being united to the resurrected Christ by faith, grounds in its entirety Paul's teaching on sanctification and the renewal of the Christian. But union with Christ as resurrected is not only renovative. That union also has judicial or forensic significance, as does Christ's own resurrection.

Paul's view, Abraham, Moses, David, and all other Old Testament believers are already justified and are, along with New Testament believers, awaiting the final judgment and with the same expectation in view.

The judicial importance of Christ's resurrection is plain from Romans 4:25, "who was delivered up for our trespasses and was raised for our justification." Here a direct connection is drawn between the resurrection and justification. In the light of the immediate and broader context of Paul's teaching, that connection is best understood as follows. As the representative sin bearer and righteous substitute (Rom. 3:25; 8:3; 2 Cor. 5:21), in his full obedience culminating in his death (Phil. 2:8), Christ's resurrection is his own justification in the sense that the resurrection is God's de facto declarative recognition, on the ground of that obedience, of his righteousness (cf. 1 Cor. 1:30). As an event, his resurrection "speaks," and it does so judicially, in a legal manner. For Christians, then, Christ's justification, given with his resurrection, becomes theirs. When they are united to the resurrected and justified Christ by faith, his righteousness is reckoned as theirs, or imputed to them.

The resurrection as Christ's own justification is confirmed by 1 Timothy 3:16, which speaks of him as "manifested in the flesh, justified in the Spirit," where the reference is almost certainly to the Holy Spirit's activity in raising Jesus from the dead. While most translations render the verb "vindicated" instead of "justified," the vindication in view is surely judicial; it is to be seen in terms of Christ's righteousness being manifested in his obedience "in the flesh," that is, during his earthly life prior to the resurrection. So there is no need or compelling reason to abandon the usual translation of the verb, "justified" (KJV, NKJV). "Shown to be righteous" (NLT) also gets at the sense. With that said, it of course needs to be kept in mind that Christ's justification, unlike the believer's, does not involve the imputation to him of the righteousness of another. The ground of his being declared righteous, unlike theirs, is his own righteousness.[4]

4. For further discussion of the resurrection as Christ's justification, see my *Resurrection and Redemption: A Study in Paul's Soteriology* (2nd ed.; Phillipsburg, NJ: P&R, 1987), esp. 119–24.

A direct connection between the believer's justification and
the resurrection is indicated in Romans 5:18 by the expression "justification of life" (*dikaiōsin zōēs*). That the reference is specifically
to the life given with Christ's resurrection is beyond doubt from
"eternal life" in verse 21 and the parallel statements in 1 Corinthians
15:21–22. The thought here is either that justification consists in life,
resurrection life as de facto justification, or, alternatively, that life
is the consequence of justification. On either understanding, and
in the light of the other passages we have noted, the resurrection is
inalienably forensic. The resurrection expounds the justification of
Christ based on his righteousness, and the believer's justification is a
function or manifestation of union with Christ in his resurrection.

Resurrection is of course meaningless apart from death; in
a standard biblical expression, it is life "from the dead" (e.g., in
Paul, Rom. 4:24; 1 Cor. 15:30; Phil. 3:11; cf. Matt. 17:9; Luke 20:35;
1 Peter 1:3). Accordingly, the forensic, justifying significance of the
resurrection we are considering is bound up with the antithetical
judicial outcome that death is. For Paul, as we saw in Chapter 2,
human death is the judicial consequence of sin. Death is neither
the merely natural outworking of sin nor the cumulative effect
of sinning. It is not only sin's own reflexive "reward" or payoff. As
the "wages of sin" (Rom. 6:23), death is not merely pecuniary, but
penal. Human death is God's response to sin, a response that is
judicial in nature. Death, as God's ultimate curse on sin, is his just
punishment of sin. Death, for Paul, is indeed inalienably penal.
Romans 5:16–18 is decisive on this point. On Adam's side of the
contrast, the central thread of the argument, as noted earlier,
does not simply go from sin to death, as the power unleashed by
sin. Rather, that thread moves from sin to condemnation and
then to death as the consequence of that condemnation, as the
explicitly judicial consequence of sin.

There is thus a forensic dimension that is essential on both
sides of the polarity between death and resurrection. Each is the
judicial consequence of, and seal on, respectively, condemna-

tion and justification. Relating that forensic dimension to the already–not yet structure of the resurrection, then, leads to this conclusion: as believers are already raised with Christ, they have been justified; as they are not yet resurrected, they are still to be justified. In terms of the anthropological profile of 2 Corinthians 4:16, "the outer man," subject to decay and wasting, mortal and destined for death, still awaits justification in some sense.

Romans 8:10 substantiates and clarifies this conclusion: "But if Christ is in you, though the body is dead because of sin, the Spirit is life because of righteousness."[5] Here Paul is considering the present situation of believers. On the one hand, and this is his primary accent, they are indwelt and enlivened by Christ through the Spirit, closely identified here with Christ as "the Spirit of Christ" (v. 9; cf. "the Spirit of life in Christ Jesus" in v. 2 and Christ as the "life-giving Spirit" in 1 Cor. 15:45). In other words, they have already been raised with Christ. But at the same time, the imprint of the dual, inner-outer anthropology of 2 Corinthians 4:16 is apparent in the way verse 10 is formulated. Expressed alternatively in the terms of 6:12–13 noted earlier, the believer is "alive from the dead" (v. 10c), but is that only "in the mortal body" (v. 10b).

In this two-sided state of affairs, on the one side the "outer," the body, is said to be "dead because of sin." That is, the body of the believer is mortal as a consequence of sin. That consequence, the believer's mortality, we are bound to say further, in the light of what we saw above in 5:16–18, is the specifically judicial consequence of sin. And on the other side, seen in terms of the "inner," it is "because of righteousness" that the Spirit is the life of the resurrected Christ indwelling the believer (cf. Gal. 2:20; Col. 3:4). The judicial ground of that life is the righteousness embodied in

5. The translation of v. 10c, "the/your spirit is alive" (e.g., NIV, NASB) can certainly be given a Pauline sense, but is not likely, if for no other reason than Paul uses the noun "life" (zōē), not an adjective ("alive"). On the exegesis of this verse, underlying my treatment here, see esp. J. Murray, *The Epistle to the Romans* (Grand Rapids: Eerdmans, 1959), 288–91.

Christ. That this consequence on the side of the "inner" is also specifically judicial is clear from "the justification of life" in 5:18, as noted above.

It is important to stress that the righteousness in view in verse 10 as the judicial ground of life—justifying righteousness, in other words—is not God's renovating work in the believer, righteousness as produced in believers. Rather, it is Christ's righteousness as distinct from theirs, from anything being done in them. If that were not the case, then Paul would be saying, in effect, "The Spirit is life because of in-wrought righteousness." But that would have things precisely backwards for him. Spirit-worked righteousness in the believer is ever the reflex or manifestation of life in the Spirit. That life is never "because of" such Spirit-produced righteousness; that righteousness is never the ground of life in the Spirit.

In order to head off potentially serious confusion and misunderstanding, I need to be clear at this point where our reflections are *not* headed. I am not arguing, in terms of the inner-outer distinction, that Paul sees the believer as only partially justified as part of an ongoing process that is not yet complete or, more importantly, uncertain as to its outcome. In the immediate context of verse 10, verse 1, like a lodestar, provides a fixed and invariable point of reference. The removal of condemnation, the justification, affirmed there is true for the whole believer, not just in part. For sinners united to Christ by faith, in the judgment rendered by God, the previously existing state of being found guilty and of being condemned has been reversed by their now being found not guilty, by their being declared just. That judicial reversal applies to the whole person in every respect. In the terms of 2 Corinthians 4:16, it is the total, single subject, the person who does not "become discouraged," who has been justified, not just "the inner man."

At the same time, however, we are bound to take into consideration the distinction—indeed, the nothing less than life-and-death *disjunction*—applied specifically to believers in verse

10, and to do so in terms of Paul's teaching on the realized–still future pattern of their resurrection. In that light, it seems fair to observe, given that for believers death is inalienably penal ("because of sin"), its removal—as the judicial consequence of the reversal of judgment already effected in justification—does not take place all at once, but unfolds in two steps, one already realized and one still future. Correlatively, the open or public declaration of that judicial reversal, that manifest declaration attendant on their bodily resurrection and the final judgment, is likewise still future. In that sense, believers are already justi-fied—by faith. But they are yet to be justified—by sight.

An illustration may help to make this point clear. The situa-tion is analogous to that of a prisoner whose conviction has been overturned and, with that reversal, his imprisonment terminated. But the procedure by which the court implements its decision, irreversible and sure in its execution, is such that the actual release from prison takes place in two stages, one immediate and the other at a point in the future (here the analogy breaks down because of the inner-outer anthropology involved). To apply the analogy, as to their inner man, sinners, when justified by faith, are instantaneously released from the prison and punishment of death; so far as their outer man is concerned, there is a delay until the resurrection in their being released from that prison.

These observations are reinforced by 1 Corinthians 15:54–56 (esv):

> When the perishable puts on the imperishable, and the mortal puts on immortality, then shall come to pass the saying that is written:
>
> > "Death is swallowed up in victory."
> > "O death, where is your victory?
> > O death, where is your sting?"
>
> The sting of death is sin, and the power of sin is the law.

Here Paul is discussing the believer's bodily resurrection, in other words, the resurrection of the "outer man."[6] In that regard (bodily resurrection), for the believer "death [being] swallowed up in victory" is not *yet* a reality. "Then"—that is, at a time still future—"shall come to pass the saying that is written: 'Death is swallowed up in victory'" (v. 54).[7] In terms of the controlling metaphor of the chapter (vv. 20, 23), so far as the Christian's place in the "harvest" of bodily resurrection is concerned, death has not yet been "swallowed up in victory."

That the church's victory over death in view here is still future is confirmed by verses 25–26. "He," that is, Christ already resurrected, "must reign *until* he has put all his enemies under his feet," with death being the "last" of these enemies "to be destroyed." Given the immediate context, the present tense of the Greek verb (*katargeitai*) plainly has a future force, as virtually all English translations recognize. By his own resurrection, the bodily resurrection of the "firstfruits," death's final and complete destruction has already occurred for him personally and so is assured for the rest of the harvest. But for them, their actual, bodily participation in that destruction has yet to occur. Further, verses 50–52 make clear that the future victory over death in verses 54–55 is at the time of the "last trumpet," that is, the final judgment (cf. 1 Thess. 4:16; Matt. 24:31).

In this setting, where the destruction of bodily death is still future for believers, verse 56 affirms, "the sting of death is sin, and the power of sin is the law." Here, with reference to the present, continuing mortality of the believer, an explicit link is made between death and sin, specifically as the latter is in view as violation of the law. Sin is "the sting of death"; it carries the "kiss" of death, we might say. That is, for believers in their bodily

6. As noted earlier, the resurrection of unbelievers is outside Paul's purview in 1 Cor. 15.

7. I leave to the side Paul's interesting use of the Old Testament here and in v. 55 (Isa. 25:8 and Hos. 13:14).

existence, sin retains its virulent, death-dealing potency and does
so, Paul says, just as the law stipulates death as the punishment
for its violation. In other words, the continuing mortality of
believers, as the consequence of sin, has legal, forensic significance. Here, we should conclude, while their bodily mortality
is certainly not seen as a sign of their continuing to be guilty
in any respect, that mortality is still in view as the present, yet
unremoved, penal consequence of sin.

To be sure, in dying for them, Christ has fully borne and
so secured the removal of the punishment that their sins justly
deserve (e.g., Rom. 3:25–26). Nothing Paul says even remotely
suggests anything else. But for them, death, as the just punishment for sin, has not yet been removed so far as the body is
concerned. For Paul, however certain death's eventual removal
for believers, to the extent that death remains and to the degree
that it is operative, the effects of punishment for sin and the
curse on it continue. In that respect, death, as punishment for
and curse on sin, is not yet removed. The culminating note of
exhortation on which the chapter ends (vv. 57–58) is consonant
with this conclusion. Paul assures Christians, "Your labors are
not in vain in the Lord," and that is true because of "God, who
gives us the victory through our Lord Jesus Christ." But, in light
of the immediately preceding verses (note the references to victory in vv. 54–55), for them that death-destroying victory, while
secured and certain, is still future.

Furthermore, these reflections do not lose sight of, nor do
they intend to eclipse, the fact that for every Christian, as for the
apostle himself, "to die is gain" (Phil. 1:21). Surely it is a provision
of God's fatherly love that the believer's bodily death becomes
the gateway to the blessing of being with Christ in a way that is
"far better" (v. 23). Death for believers is the means of access to
the perfecting of the "inner man," with the burdens of present,
mortal bodily existence left behind. Also, Christians, body as well
as soul, remain united to Christ even in death. This appears to

be a fair inference from 1 Thessalonians 4:14, "For if we believe that Jesus died and rose again, even so God will bring with him those who have fallen asleep in Jesus."[8]

Further, nothing, not even death itself, can separate them from the love of God in Christ (Rom. 8:38–39). For them, though they are still presently subject to death as the penalty for sin, God is no longer a wrathful and unreconciled judge, but their loving, heavenly Father. Suffering and bodily dying do remain present realities for them because of their sinfulness in Adam (Rom. 5:12–21) and their consequent corruption and active complicity in sinning that continue until death. Yet God will, in the words of the hymn, "sanctify to [them their] deepest distress." In fact, in an important strand of Paul's teaching that I am unable to take up here, for believers "the sufferings of the present time" (Rom. 8:18) can and do also become an expression of their already having been raised with Christ.[9]

Still, bodily death, though a transition to greater blessing, is not as such, in itself, a blessing. In expressing a preference to be "away from the body and at home with the Lord" (2 Cor. 5:8), Paul at the same time recoils, with intensity ("we groan"), from the ultimate "nakedness" this disembodied existence involves, and to be spared such disembodiment is his deep desire (vv. 2–4).[10] For the creature made bodily in God's image and awaiting in hope the full restoration of that image in the resurrection of the body (1 Cor. 15:49), to be deprived of bodily existence is a

8. On the basis of this verse, Westminster Shorter Catechism 37 speaks of the dead bodies of believers as "being still united to Christ"; similarly, Westminster Larger Catechism 86 speaks of "waiting for the full redemption of their bodies [Rom. 8:23], which even in death continue united to Christ [1 Thess. 4:14]."

9. See esp. 2 Cor. 4:10–11; Phil. 3:10; cf. 2 Cor. 12:9–10; Phil. 1:29. For a discussion of these and related passages, primarily in Paul, see my "The Usefulness of the Cross," *Westminster Theological Journal* 41 (1978–79): 228–46.

10. On the interpretation of these verses, see esp. G. Vos, *The Pauline Eschatology* (1930; Grand Rapids: Baker, 1979), 186–98.

deep and distorting abnormality, which has its only adequate explanation in death as the judicial consequence of sin. To view the bodily death of believers, their experience of dying itself, less starkly or more positively than the death of unbelievers is to be on the way to romanticizing death in a way that is foreign to Paul—and, for that matter, the rest of the biblical writers. God's love for believers is not manifested in death as such, but in sustaining them, despite death, in the unbroken fellowship of his fatherly love and care (cf. Rom. 8:38–39), until this last vestige of the wages of sin is removed in the resurrection of the body.

To summarize, the "outer man" of the believer does not yet experience the saving benefits of union with Christ, either transformative or forensic. So far as I am "outer man," I am not yet justified (openly), any more than I am resurrected (bodily). And that is so, without diminishing either the reality that I am already and irreversibly justified or the future certainty of my being justified in the resurrection of the body at the final judgment. Here again, in terms of the principle of 2 Corinthians 5:7, I am justified "by faith," but not (yet) "by sight."

Adoption. This conclusion regarding the present-future structure of the Christian's justification is confirmed by an aspect of Paul's teaching on adoption. Like justification, adoption in Paul is a forensic reality. Briefly, human beings, as sinners alienated from God, are not naturally his sons. Quite the opposite, they are "by nature children of [his] wrath" (Eph. 2:3). This divine wrath is inalienably judicial; it is always his just wrath (Rom. 2:5, 8; 2 Thess. 1:8–9). Accordingly, removal of that wrath and restoration to fellowship with God as his sons has a legal aspect. Christians are not God's sons either inherently or by virtue of creation. Neither is that identity the outcome of a renovative process. Rather, the believer has the status of being God's son by his decisive, declarative act. Adoption, like justification, is judicially declarative.

In Romans 8:14–17, Paul is emphatically clear that believers have already been adopted. They are now, by adoption, "sons of God," and among the consequent privileges they enjoy, the Spirit who indwells them is "the Spirit of adoption," assuring them that now, presently, God is their Father and they, as his adopted sons, may address him as such.

But then, just a few verses later, we read: "We wait eagerly for adoption, the redemption of our bodies" (v. 23). Now adoption is future, at the time of the resurrection; it is given with or realized in bodily resurrection. Here, too, for adoption, as we saw to be the case for justification, the future resurrection of the body is invested with de facto forensic significance. The resurrection of believers will be declarative of their adoption.

Within basically the same context, the scope of a few verses, then, adoption as a forensic, declarative reality is seen as both present and future. Initially this could seem confusing, even incoherent. How can it be both? By the nature of the case, it would seem apparent, either I am adopted or I am not. If I am adopted, how can I be awaiting adoption?

Paul, we can be sure, is not involved here in some kind of double-talk. He is not speaking in paradox, with adoption as future rendering uncertain adoption as present and settled. The left hand of the "not yet" of adoption does not take away or cancel out in dialectical fashion what the right hand of the "already" of adoption gives. Rather, the respect in which he distinguishes present and future is clear from the immediate context. What is still future is what the entire creation longs for: "the revelation of the sons of God," which we may fairly gloss as "the *open* revelation of the sons of God" (v. 19). Again, what is in prospect is "the freedom of the glory of the children of God," the free and open manifestation of their glory (v. 21). Believers await the open manifestation of their adoption in the resurrection of the body.

Here, again, the principle of 2 Corinthians 5:7 is present and controlling. For now, until Jesus comes, Christians have their adoption "by faith," but not yet "by sight." They are God's adopted children in the mode of "believing," but not (yet) of "seeing." It is in fact the case that they are not yet openly adopted. A fair commentary on Paul at this point is 1 John 3:2, "Now we are the children of God, and what we will be has not yet been revealed."

Paul's statements on adoption, we may conclude, provide a window on how he would have us view the closely related forensic blessing of justification. As adoption is both present and future, so too is justification. We have already been justified by faith, but not (yet) by sight. Akin to our adoption, our justification has still to be made public or openly manifested. We have not yet been "openly acquitted."

The Final Judgment. While explicit references in Paul to justification as future may be minimal and debatable, in several places he either speaks of or clearly indicates the relevance of the final judgment for Christians and says that, as it includes them, it will be a judgment "according to works." That is, as we will see, at the final judgment "works" will serve as an essential criterion.

The clearest passages in this regard are Romans 2:5-16 and 2 Corinthians 5:10.[11] The latter is the capstone declaration of a section (vv. 1-10) where, as already noted, Paul speaks of the penultimate hope of Christians, the hope of being present with the Lord apart from the body at death. His primary interest, however, is their ultimate hope of bodily resurrection. "For we must all appear before the judgment seat of Christ, so that each one may receive what is due for the things he has done in the body, whether good or evil." Believers, too, face final judgment, and for them, too, that judgment will involve the just adjudication of the things they have done bodily, in "the outer man."

In Romans, Paul is intent in the first major section primarily on establishing the universality of human sin (1:18–3:20). His basic assessment is summarized, just beyond this section, in

---

11. See as well Acts 17:31; Rom. 14:10; 2 Tim. 4:1.

the words of 3:23, that "there is no distinction" between Jews, despite their privileged possession of the law, and non-Jews, "for all have sinned and fall short of the glory of God." In the course of this argument, reference is made in 2:5 to "the day of wrath and revelation of God's righteous judgment," and verse 6 adds that on that judgment day "he will render to each one according to his works,"[12] with verses 7–11 detailing the two sides of the judgment in view with their respective outcomes.

Do verses 5–11, on their positive side, have in view a scenario that is actual or one that is unrealized and true only in principle? Is Paul describing Christians and the actual outcome of the final judgment for them, or is he speaking hypothetically? The former reading is almost certainly right. For the hypothetical view, that Paul is speaking of what is true in principle and does not have in view the actual conduct of any sinful human being, Christians included, one of the main arguments advanced is that reference in these verses to the gospel or to provisions and consequences of the gospel is lacking and furthermore would be foreign to the larger context (1:18–3:20), where Paul's concern is with the law and sin as universal; not until 3:21 and following does he begin to discuss the gospel and salvation, in particular justification by faith without the works of the law.

As a generalization, there is a large element of truth in this "pre-evangelical" view of 1:18–3:20. But it is subject to certain qualifications, and these have a bearing on how to understand 2:5–11. For instance, in 2:29 "circumcision of the heart, in the Spirit," marking the one who is a Jew "inwardly," can hardly be read other than as a reference to those in a saving covenant relationship with God and so would include Christians. That is supported, if not put beyond question, by the description of the church in Philippians 3:3 as "the [true] circumcision, who worship by the Spirit of God and glory in Christ Jesus and are not confident in the flesh."

12. Quoting from the Greek OT, Ps. 61:13 (Hebrew, 62:13; English, 62:12) and Prov. 24:12; cf. Eccl. 12:14.

In other words, Paul's argumentation is such that an outcome of the gospel, and an important one at that, is in view prior to 3:21. Also, and even more directly related to 2:6–13, the final judgment, just as it is in view in these verses, is, Paul says, "according to my gospel" (v. 16). Paul apparently sees the positive side of the judgment described in verses 5–11 as involving "good news," as having not just legal but gospel significance.

Another major argument raised against the view that this passage on its positive side is about the final judgment for Christians is that to take it that way, especially if verses 12 and 13 are included, creates a contradiction with Paul's clear and consistent teaching elsewhere that justification is not by works but by faith. Pointedly, it is argued, to apply to Christians the latter half of verse 13, "The doers of the law . . . will be justified," flatly contradicts 3:20, "By the works of the law no one will be justified in his [God's] sight," and many other like passages. However, as I hope our discussion will show, even if verse 13b is properly applied to believers—likely the case, but which I leave an open question here—contradiction need not be the result.

The hypothetical reading of verses 5–13, or at least verses 5–11, is beset with a substantial difficulty. The future judgment in view here, including the principle or role of works involved, is no different from the descriptions or allusions we find in a number of places elsewhere in Scripture. The following may be cited among such New Testament passages.[13]

> For the Son of Man will come with his angels in the glory of his Father, and then he will repay each person according to his works. (Matt. 16:27)

> For an hour is coming when all who are in the tombs will hear his voice and come out, those who have done good to the

---

13. For the OT, e.g., in addition to the references cited in n. 12, see Job 34:11; Jer. 17:10, 32:19.

resurrection of life and those who have done evil to the resurrection of judgment. (John 5:28–29)

[Before the great white throne, picturing the final judgment,] the dead were judged by what was written in the books, according to their works. (Rev. 20:13)

I am coming soon, and my reward is with me, to repay everyone according to his work. (Rev. 22:12)

And Paul, in exhorting believers not to grow weary in doing what is good, says:

For whatever one sows, that will he also reap. For the one who sows to his own flesh will from the flesh reap corruption, but the one who sows to the Spirit will from the Spirit reap eternal life. (Gal. 6:7–9, ESV)

If Romans 2:5–13 is interpreted hypothetically, then the perceived problem of conflict with biblical teaching on justification by faith simply defaults to these and similar passages, and they will also have to be interpreted hypothetically on their positive side. But consideration of them will show, as John Murray puts it bluntly, "the impossibility of such a procedure."[14] The broader biblical context suggests that the positive outcome in view in Romans 2:5–13, at least in verses 5–11, if not verses 12–13 as well, is best seen as describing what will be true of Christians at the final judgment.

Looking now within this passage, it is apparent that on its positive side, for Christians, what is at issue is not some penultimate outcome—say, relative degrees or levels of reward, as this and related passages are sometimes understood. Rather, as is

14. Murray, *Romans*, 63. Among the vast commentary and monograph literature on this passage, Murray's treatment remains particularly helpful and has especially shaped my own approach.

clear on the negative side, at stake is final judgment in nothing less than its ultimate issue: all-or-nothing, final, eternal destiny. This is apparent from the way verses 6–11 are composed. God's impartiality as judge in verses 6 and 11 is the idea that brackets an a-b-b-a chiasm, with verse 10 corresponding to verse 7, and verse 9 to verse 8.

On the positive side, for "those who by perseverance in doing good [good work] seek glory, honor, and immortality" (v. 7), for "everyone who does [works] what is good" (v. 10), both Jews and Greeks, the outcome of the judgment in view is "eternal life" (v. 7), "glory and honor and peace" (v. 10), an outcome that stands in unrelieved antithesis to the only other alternative in view: eternal destruction, described as "wrath and fury," "anguish and distress," as the ultimate outcome for the self-willed and disobedient, whether Jew or Greek (vv. 8–9).

Within the larger context of Paul's teaching as a whole, then, the question is unavoidable. How are we to relate this future judgment according to works, as spelled out in this passage and others, to his clear and emphatic teaching elsewhere that justification, as already pronounced eschatological judgment, is a present reality, received by faith alone and on the sole basis of the imputed righteousness of God revealed in Christ?

The answer to this relational question does not lie in the direction of distinguishing two different justifications. This view has variant forms: one present, by faith, and one future, by works; or, present justification by faith alone, and future justification by faith plus works, the former based on Christ's work and the latter based on our works, whether or not seen as Spirit-empowered; or, yet again, present justification based on faith in anticipation of future justification on the basis of a lifetime of faithfulness.[15]

15. The latter is the view, e.g., of N. T. Wright: "Present justification declares, on the basis of faith, what future justification will affirm publicly (according to [Rom.] 2:14–16 and 8:9–11) on the basis of the entire life" (*What Saint Paul Really Said* [Grand Rapids: Eerdmans, 1997], 129).

Rather, the answer lies where by now we should expect to find it, in the already–not yet structure of union with Christ by faith and in the nature of that faith, particularly as "faith working through love" (Gal. 5:6). There can be little question that this is a description of justifying faith. This is so in view of the immediate context, where the issue is whether circumcision is necessary for justification (vv. 2–6), and given the terms of the contrast within verse 6 ("neither circumcision nor uncircumcision counts for anything, but faith working through love").

For Christians, future judgment according to works does not operate according to a different principle than their already having been justified by faith. The difference is that the final judgment will be the open manifestation of that present justification, their being "openly acquitted," as we have seen. And in that future judgment, their good works will not be the ground or basis of their acquittal. Nor are they (co-)instrumental, a coordinate instrument for appropriating divine approbation as they supplement faith. Rather, they are the essential and manifest criterion of that faith, the integral "fruits and evidences of a true and lively faith," appropriating the language of the Westminster Confession of Faith, 16.2. It is not for nothing, and not to be dismissed as drawing too fine a distinction exegetically to observe, that in Romans 2:6 Paul writes "according to (*kata*) works," not "on account of (*dia*) works" (which would express the ground) nor "by (*ek*) works" (which would express the instrument).[16]

Resurrection and Final Judgment. Toward the beginning of our discussion of justification as future, we cited the two catechism answers from the Westminster Standards that speak of believers being openly acquitted at the final judgment. The ques-

---

16. Among the vast literature on this passage and the issues it raises, particularly helpful are H. Ridderbos, *Paul: An Outline of His Theology* (trans. J. R. de Witt; Grand Rapids: Eerdmans, 1975), 178–81 ("Judgment according to Works") and the concluding observations of Murray, *Romans*, 78–79.

tions, readers may have noted, differ. Larger Catechism 90 asks, "What shall be done to the righteous at *the day of judgment*?" Shorter Catechism 38 reads, "What benefits do believers receive from Christ *at the resurrection*?" (italics added). These different phrasings raise the question how bodily resurrection and final judgment are related. So far as Paul is concerned, it seems clear (as Larger Catechism 88 affirms), especially in the light of 2 Corinthians 5:10, that the resurrection precedes the final judgment. In other words, believers, in union with Christ, will appear at the final judgment as already resurrected bodily. That is, they will appear there in "spiritual," that is, Spirit-enlivened and Spirit-transformed bodies marked by imperishability, glory, and power (1 Cor. 15:42–44) and as they are already fully conformed to the image of their firstborn brother, the exalted Christ (v. 49; cf. Rom. 8:29).

This carries an implication, as important as it is obvious, for understanding and for ministering Paul's teaching on justification as future. If believers appear at the final judgment as already resurrected bodily, then they will appear there as *already openly justified*. Their future justification, as we have been speaking of it, will have already taken place in their resurrection, with the de facto declarative, forensic, justifying significance it has in Paul, as we have pointed out above. That means, further, that for believers the final judgment, as it is to be according to works, will have for them a reality that will, as we have already noted, reflect and further attest their justification, which has been openly manifested in their bodily resurrection.

It would be perverse, then, to read Paul's teaching on the final judgment, as well as my discussion of it here, as leaving believers in this life, in the face of death, uncertain of the future—unable to know for sure the outcome for them at the final judgment and wondering whether they have produced enough "good works" in this life for a favorable verdict at that point entitling them to eternal life. To the contrary, everything at stake here, including their assurance, depends on Christ—specifically, if it needs to be said again, his finished righteousness, imputed to them and received by faith alone. At the same time, Paul's teaching on the final judgment and the role it will have for believers does put in ultimate perspective the integral, unbreakable bond he sees between justification and sanctification, and the truth that faith as "the alone instrument of justification . . . is . . . not alone in the person justified" (Westminster Confession of Faith 11.2).

Faith and Obedience

Paul's teaching on the final judgment, as judgment according to works, prompts some further comment, beyond what we have already noted toward the close of Chapter 3, on the perennial and much-debated question of how he sees the relationship between faith and the believer's obedience, or good works. That question needs to be properly focused, which we can do here in terms of the distinction between law and gospel. A law-gospel antithesis is certainly present in Paul, but ought not to be so construed or overextended that the result is a polarization in every respect between believing and doing, or, as can too often happen, an uneasy tension in the life of those justified between grace and faith on the one hand and "works" on the other.

Such a polarization cuts at the heart of Paul's understanding of salvation and at an even more foundational level of his theology, the positive relationship he sees between creation and redemption. In ultimate perspective, God's electing purpose culminates in conformity to the image of his Son (Rom. 8:29). Despite the entrance of sin and its distorting consequences (Rom. 5:12–21), God's original purposes for his image bearers at creation have been realized in the glorified Christ (1 Cor. 15:44b–49)—the true, because consummate, image of God (Col. 1:15). His eternal intention is that those united to Christ by faith may bear his transforming image—now presently and partially (2 Cor. 3:18) and consummately at his return (1 Cor. 15:49; cf. Phil. 3:21). To be in the image of God is, by design, to be found doing his will, to live before him in trusting and dependent obedience to his commands. That is clear, by contrast, from the negative description of human sin and disobedience in Romans 1:21–32. Doing God's will is essential to the divine image as originally created in Adam and restored in Christ.

This positive construal of human doing hardly involves concurring with those, past and present, who limit in some way the scope of "(the) works (of the law)" that Paul so resolutely opposes for justification. Most recently, the New Perspective, at least for the most part, began by narrowing these works to "boundary markers" of Jewish ethnic identity, like circumcision, food laws, and the Sabbath. Now that the exegetical untenability of that narrowing has become apparent, that position has been modified so that this opposition is seen to be against the entire Mosaic law, but still only as it functions as such a national identity marker. The Reformation, I take it, has gotten Paul's polemic against works right, at its crucial, decisive point. He is against any and all human effort, including distorted notions of faith, offered to achieve or maintain the ground for a justified status before God. Ephesians 2:8–9 and Titus 3:5–7, for instance, make that clear.

In the lives of those justified by faith, however, there is a positive or synthetic relationship between faith and works, a constructive bond between faith and what faith does. Probably the most instructive single passage in Paul in this respect is one just alluded to, Ephesians 2:8–9, together with verse 10. There, within one brief unit of discourse, the vocabulary of "works" is used in two opposed, even antithetical, senses. "Works" are both the enemy of grace and the fruit of grace. On the one hand (vv. 8–9), saving grace through faith clearly stands implacably opposed to "works"; that is, grace cuts off every effort—Pelagian, semi-Pelagian, or any other—at self-salvation, all attempts to secure or retain salvation on the basis of one's status and/or accomplishments. Here an absolute antithesis between law and gospel is clear and pointed. Yet on the other hand, and at the same time and inseparably (v. 10), grace just as clearly functions as the power of the new creation in Christ to produce "good works."

Instructive here as well is the way Paul captures this bond with the expression "the obedience of faith" (Rom. 1:5; 16:26). This phrase, occurring at both the beginning and end of Romans— its "bookends," we may say—brackets its teaching as a whole. Furthermore, it clearly does so as it indicates the bottom-line response that Paul is seeking to his gospel as summarized in both 1:2–4 and 16:25. The response to the gospel that he is intent on "among all the Gentiles," as well as the Jews, is, all told, "the obedience of faith."

In this expression, "of faith"[17] is best taken as intentionally multivalent.[18] In relation to "obedience," it is appositional and also indicates source or origin. In other words, in view is faith itself as an act of obedience (cf. Acts 16:31), together with other acts of obedience that stem from faith. Doubtful at best is the view—in effect, a reversal of the traditional appositional understanding—that equates faith with faithfulness or obedience, understood as covenantal fidelity or loyalty.[19] If that were what Paul had intended to say (faithfulness that consists in obedience),

17. In the genitive case in the Greek text, *hypakoē pisteōs*.

18. D. B. Garlington, *Faith, Obedience, and Perseverance: Aspects of Paul's Letter to the Romans* (Tübingen: J. C. B. Mohr, 1994), 30: "In Rom 1:5 (16:26), Paul has chosen to coin an *ambiguous* phrase expressive of two ideas: the obedience which consists in faith and the obedience which is the product of faith" (italics original). For a more extensive treatment of this phrase, see R. B. Gaffin, Jr., "The Obedience of Faith," in *Israel and the Church: Essays in Honour of Allan Macdonald Harman on His 65th Birthday and Retirement*, ed. D. Milne (Melbourne: Theological Education Committee, Presbyterian Church of Victoria, 2001), 71–85.

19. Apparently the view, e.g., of N. T. Wright, "The Letter to the Romans: Introduction, Commentary, and Reflections," in *The New Interpreter's Bible*, vol. 10 (Nashville: Abingdon Press, 2002), 420 ("This faith is actually the human faithfulness that answers to God's faithfulness"; cf. "the response of human faithfulness," in arguing for translating 1:17, "the righteous shall live by faithfulness").

he might well have written, "the faith of obedience." Whatever validity there may be to that surmise, more important and decisive is a categorical description like Galatians 5:6, "faith working through love." Here, the two are closely associated, but faith is plainly distinguished from faithfulness or faithful obedience. The latter, focused here in loving, is not identical with faith, but its fruit or result.

The closest equivalents to the expression elsewhere in Paul appear to be 1 Thessalonians 1:3, "your work of faith" ("your work produced by faith," NIV) and 2 Thessalonians 1:11, "every . . . work of faith" ("every act prompted by your faith," NIV). The outcome targeted by the gospel is a life marked by "the obedience of faith," the new creation good works (Eph. 2:10), wrought in believers as attendant expressions of their saving faith. For Paul, faith and works, that is, an extraspective trust in and reliance on Christ, as an act of obedience, and other acts of obedience are distinct from each other but inseparable. In fact, we may say, faith and good works, thus distinguished, are always synecdochic. To speak of the one invariably has the other in view; they are unintelligible apart from each other. They always exist without confusion, yet inseparably. James 2:18, "Show me your faith without your works, and I will show you my faith by my works"—which admits of no exceptions for those in restored fellowship, by faith, with God—is a fair commentary on Paul in this regard.

From this perspective, it should be appreciated that the antithesis between law and gospel is not an end in itself. It is not a theological ultimate. That antithesis arises not by virtue of creation, but as the consequence of sin, and the gospel functions to overcome it. The gospel removes an absolute law-gospel antithesis in the life of the believer. How so? Briefly, apart from the gospel and outside of Christ, the law is my enemy and condemns me. Why? Because *God* is my enemy and condemns me. But with the gospel and in Christ, united to him by faith, the law is no longer my enemy but my friend. Why? Because now *God* is no longer my enemy but my friend, and the law, *his* will—the law in its moral core, as reflective of his character and of concerns eternally inherent in his own person and so of what pleases him—is now my friendly guide for life in fellowship with God.

Paul and James

These observations on faith and obedience may be reinforced by referring here briefly to the perennial debate over Paul and James on faith and works and what is sometimes taken to be their contradictory teaching on justification. On the coherence between them, it is hard to improve on what J. Gresham Machen writes aphoristically, "As the faith which James condemns is different than the faith that Paul commends, so also the works which James commends are different than the works which Paul condemns."[20] Further, as Machen also recognizes, an important reconciling link, "the solution to the whole problem . . . in a single phrase," is Paul's own characterization of justifying faith in Galatians 5:6 as "faith working through love."[21] Elsewhere he writes, "The faith that Paul means when he speaks of justification by faith alone is a faith that works."[22]

Conversely, as was just noted, but bears repeating, Paul, the apostle of "the obedience of faith," is in full agreement with James 2:18, "Show me your faith apart from your works [which you can't], and I will show you my faith by my works" (ESV)—an assertion unqualified and not to be qualified, a principle that holds always and at every point for life in reconciled fellowship with God. In this regard, it is hardly gratuitous to suggest that the Abraham of James 2:21–24, as well as anyone, exemplifies the

20. J. G. Machen, *The New Testament: An Introduction to Its Literature and History* (ed. W. J. Cook; Edinburgh: Banner of Truth, 1976), 239.
21. It is noteworthy that at least here Machen does not seek the solution in different senses in Paul and James for the verb *justify*.
22. J. G. Machen, *What Is Faith?* (London: Hodder & Stoughton, 1925), 204 (in a chapter on "Faith and Works," worth reading in its entirety).

response of Romans 1:5 to the gospel promise of the covenant that was eventually fulfilled in Christ (vv. 2–4), the response of "the obedience of faith." This Abraham, the Abraham of the obedience of faith, implicitly brackets and so qualifies everything Paul says about him and his faith elsewhere in Romans. In fact, we may say, in Romans we in effect meet the Abraham of James both in 1:5, before Abraham is introduced explicitly in chapter 4, and also after that, in 16:26. These two are not somehow different persons, nor does each function as a theological construct in tension with the other. They are one and the same, and we can never properly understand one without the other.

These observations are not only indications of agreement between Paul and James. Looking beyond the teaching of the New Testament, they carry a perennially important reminder for the life of the church. Disaster will surely result from denying or obscuring faith as "the alone instrument of justification," both present and future. But such faith "is not alone in the person justified, but . . . is no dead faith, but works by love," to utilize the balanced expression of the Westminster Confession of Faith, 11.2. The church does justice to Paul's message of justification by faith alone only when, like the apostle, it maintains that balance: the alone instrument that is never alone.

Paul does not teach a "faith alone" position, as I have sometimes heard it put. Rather, his is a "by faith alone" position. This is not just a verbal quibble; the "by" is all-important here. The faith by which sinners are justified, as it unites them to Christ and so secures for them all the benefits of salvation that there are in him, perseveres to the end and in persevering is never alone. Faith is, as Luther is reported to have said, "a busy little thing."[23]

23. The actual statement, from his preface to Romans (1522/1546), reads, "O it is a living, busy, active, mighty thing, this faith. It is impossible for it not to be doing good works incessantly" (*Luther's Works*, vol. 35, ed. E. T. Bachmann [*Word and Sacrament*, vol. 1; Philadelphia: Fortress Press, 1959], 370). I am indebted to Tom Brouwer for his initiative in contacting me with this statement and supplying its documentation.

Justification and the Present

These reflections on justification and eschatology in Paul and on what we have seen to be the attendant already–not yet structure of his teaching on justification, including what he teaches about the final judgment, may be reinforced by briefly inquiring into how he relates justification to the believer's present and the ongoing circumstances of the Christian life. That inquiry may be facilitated, once again, by a couple of references from the history of theology. The Westminster Confession of Faith, in affirming that God continues to forgive the sins of those justified, speaks of their being in "the state of justification," a state from which "they can never fall" (11.5). This mode of expression points to the present significance of justification for believers—its ongoing, daily relevance for their lives. It also prompts the question how it is that those already justified are sustained in that state and kept infallibly from falling away from it. In a similar vein, Calvin, in the course of his lengthy treatment of justification in Book 3 of his *Institutes of the Christian Religion* (chapters 11–18), entitles chapter 14, "The Beginning of Justification and its Continual Progress." There he also writes, "Therefore, we must have this blessedness [justification] not just once but must hold to it throughout life."[24]

Our concern here is not to explore further either of these references, Calvin or the Westminster Confession, but to note that the idiom used by each is faithful to Paul. That is clear, notably, in Romans 8:33–34. The discourse in this chapter, which peaks to its final crescendo in verses 38–39, begins its final section with rhetorical questions in verse 31: "What then shall we say to these things? If God is for us, who can be against us?" In the latter question, "for us" and "against us" likely at least include a

24. J. Calvin, *Institutes of the Christian Religion* (trans. F. L. Battles; ed. J. T. McNeill; Library of Christian Classics; 2 vols.; Philadelphia: Westminster, 1960), 1:778 (3.14.11).

legal or forensic overtone. They suggest a judicial proceeding, in fact one taking place in the present. Such a judicial scenario is beyond question in the related questions that begin verses 33 and 34, respectively: "Who will bring any charge against God's elect?" and "Who is the one that condemns?" Plainly, issues that concern justification are at stake here.

These questions receive their answer in the synthetic parallelism between the latter halves of these verses. First, "God is the one who justifies" (v. 33). That is decisive; it settles the issue. Verse 34b, then, explicates the justifying activity of God as it is in view here: "Christ Jesus is the one who died—more than that, who was raised, who also is at the right hand of God, who also is interceding for us." In a word, Christ is the one who expounds God as justifier.

Noteworthy for the issue we are concerned with here is how, according to verse 34, Christ is said to be relevant, even decisive, for justification and its maintenance. His death is mentioned first, and our reaction may well be, "Yes, of course." Paul has made that abundantly clear already in Romans, for instance in 3:24–26; 5:9, 18–19, as well as in the unmistakable allusion in this passage in verse 32 ("he who did not spare his own Son but gave him up for us all"): the obedience of Christ, culminating in his propitiatory death, is the righteousness that grounds the believer's justification.

But here Paul does not stop with his death. In the matter of Christ's work that is pertinent to our justification, he does not punctuate his reference to Christ's death with a period. "More than that . . .," he continues. Is more than Christ's death, past and definitive as it is, integral to our justification and even necessary for it? "Yes" is Paul's apparent answer, for he goes on to speak of his resurrection with its enduring consequences. He points his readers to what is presently the case, and in this passage at least that is where his emphasis lies: on the continuing intercessory presence of the resurrected Christ at God's right hand "for us."

For Paul, justification is bound up with this ongoing intercessory presence, in the sense that our remaining, infallibly, in
"the state of justification"—our not being separated from the
love of God in Christ, not even by death or whatever the future
brings (vv. 38–39)—depends upon this continuing and unfailing
intercession. Christ, exalted to God's right hand, is the exhibi-
tion of that finished and perfect righteousness that is ours as
it is reckoned as ours. So, his presence in that place of ultimate
and final judgment, as the righteousness which he "became for
us . . . from God" (1 Cor. 1:30), is the permanently effective answer
to any charge brought against already justified believers—that
"answer," it should not be missed, that is provided by God the
Father out of his great love for the elect (v. 32). Christ is the living embodiment of that righteousness that has been irrevocably
imputed to believers, and as such he continues to avail for the
justification of God's already justified elect (v. 30) in the sense
that he sustains them in their justified state. And he does that
sustaining work with unwavering faithfulness, just as he, their
righteousness, has and ever will, ever since each of those elect
was first united to him by faith. Because of his intercession, they
cannot and will not ever fall from "the state of justification."[25]

25. For some expansion of these comments on Romans 8:33–34, see my
"'More Than That'—Christ's Exaltation and Justification," in *The People's
Theologian: Writings in Honour of Donald Macleod*, ed. I. D. Campbell and M.
Maclean (Fearn, UK: Mentor/Christian Focus, 2011), 139–45.

Epilogue

THESE REFLECTIONS on the order of salvation in Paul may be given a final focus with some observations prompted by Colossians 1:27, with its evocative description, "Christ in you, the hope of glory." Writing at a later point in his ministry, Paul, in the immediate context (vv. 24–29), is reflecting back on that ministry as a whole. That Christ is central in these reflections is hardly unexpected, but just how he is highlighted is noteworthy. He is the "mystery . . . revealed" (v. 26)—the revelation, the realization now, finally, at last of the previously hidden salvation purposed by God from eternity. Within the wider context, he is "the first-born from the dead," and by God's good pleasure "the fullness of deity" indwells him "bodily" (vv. 18–19; 2:9). Christ, now exalted by virtue of his death and resurrection, is the full embodiment of who God is. He is "Christ in you, the hope of glory."

Christ is in view here for who he now is because of the unfolding of redemptive history to its consummation. At the same time and just as clearly, he is present with the church and indwelling believers. In other words, the Christ of the *historia salutis* consummated is the Christ of the *ordo salutis*—Christ as he is actually appropriated in salvation, "Christ in you, the hope of glory."

This prompts a question. Why in the Reformation and evangelical tradition does this description not play more of a role than it appears to have played? How often, when asked about our hope of glory, about our confidence for future eschatological blessing, for our entrance into and possession of that consummate beatitude at Christ's return, do we hear or give Paul's answer—as it is properly personalized, without denying or losing sight of its corporate aspect—"Christ in me"? That question is all the more appropriate because at issue here in this hope is nothing less or other than "the hope of the *gospel*" (v. 23).

Perhaps I should be more cautious here and not speak too broadly. It does seem to me, however, that typically in the Reformation tradition the hope of salvation is expressed in terms of the free forgiveness of sins or, if theologized further, in terms of Christ's imputed righteousness, active and passive. I beg not to be misunderstood here. As I hope I have already made clear repeatedly in this book, the New Perspective notwithstanding, that way of speaking to express confidence of salvation is surely faithful to Paul.

At the same time, however, I wonder if "Christ in you" is not more prominent as an expression of evangelical hope because our vision is too limited and we see in this description only the transforming Christ, Christ who by his Spirit is at work in the believer. With that limitation we are aware, as we must be, how that transforming work is one that is in progress at best and incomplete, flawed by our continued sinning, a work of ongoing renewal that, considered in itself, hardly provides a stable basis for hope in the face of final judgment.

I wonder, too, if at work as well is the tendency, discussed earlier, to talk about justification without appreciating that and how it is a manifestation of union with Christ—the tendency to detach the participatory and the forensic, union and justification, and to do so in a way that depreciates or even eclipses union or views union, because mystical and spiritual, as only involving sanctification and renewal.

But for Paul, we should be clear, Christ, who by his Spirit indwells believers and is conforming them to his image, is manifestly the *whole* Christ. As he has become, all told, saving "wisdom from God to us," he is our "righteousness and sanctification" (I Cor. 1:30). In him, both our justification and our sanctification, though not to be confused with each other, are inseparable and given together. In other words, as we may put it with an eye to our discussion of the present aspect of justification toward the close of the previous chapter, the Christ of Colossians 1:27 is none other than the Christ of Romans 8:34. As indwelling, he is more than transforming. As he is here, in us, intent on conforming us to his image by his Spirit, he is also there, at God's right hand, our righteousness, faithfully interceding for us. Christ "in us" is also and ever Christ "for us." He is in us only as he is also for us, and he is for us only as he is also in us.

"Christ in you, the hope of glory." There can hardly be a better or more appropriate ending to these reflections on the order of salvation in Paul, centered as that salvation is in the Christian's union with Christ, than this, his confident note of apostolic hope.

Bibliography

Allert, C. D. *A High View of Scripture?* Grand Rapids: Baker Academic, 2007.

Bavinck, H. *Gereformeerde Dogmatiek*. Kampen: Kok, 1976. Translated by John Vriend as *Reformed Dogmatics* (Grand Rapids: Baker, 2006).

Berkouwer, G. C. *Faith and Sanctification*. Translated by J. Vriend. Grand Rapids: Eerdmans, 1952.

Calvin, J. *Institutes of the Christian Religion*. Translated by F. L. Battles. Edited by J. T. McNeill. 2 vols. Library of Christian Classics. Philadelphia: Westminster, 1960.

Campbell, C. R. *Paul and Union with Christ: An Exegetical and Theological Study*. Grand Rapids: Zondervan, 2012.

Dabney, R. *Systematic Theology*. 1871. Edinburgh: Banner of Truth, n.d.

Dunn, J. D. G. "The New Perspective on Paul." *Bulletin of the John Rylands Library* 65 (1983): 95–122.

———. "The New Perspective on Paul: Whence, What, Whither?" In *The New Perspective on Paul: Collected Essays*, 1–88. Tübingen: Mohr Siebeck, 2005.

———. *The Theology of Paul the Apostle*. Grand Rapids: Eerdmans, 1998.

Fisher, J. *The Assembly's Shorter Catechism Explained, by Way of Question and Answer*. Glasgow: William Smith, 1779.

Flavel, J. *An Exposition of the Assembly's Shorter Catechism*. In *The Whole Works of the Reverend Mr. John Flavel*. Edinburgh: Andrew Anderson, 1701.

Gaffin, R. B., Jr. "The Last Adam, the Life-Giving Spirit." In *The Forgotten Christ: Exploring the Majesty and Mystery of God Incarnate*, edited by S. Clark, 191–231. Nottingham: Apollos, 2007.

———. "'Life-Giving Spirit': Probing the Center of Paul's Pneumatology." *Journal of the Evangelical Theological Society* 41.4 (December 1998): 573–89.

———. "'More Than That'—Christ's Exaltation and Justification." In *The People's Theologian: Writings in Honour of Donald Macleod*, edited by I. D. Campbell and M. Maclean, 139–45. Fearn, UK: Mentor/Christian Focus, 2011.

———. "The Obedience of Faith." In *Israel and the Church: Essays in Honour of Allan Macdonald Harman on His 65th Birthday and Retirement*, edited by D. Milne, 71–85. Melbourne: Theological Education Committee, Presbyterian Church of Victoria, 2001.

———. *Resurrection and Redemption: A Study in Paul's Soteriology.* 2nd ed. Phillipsburg, NJ: P&R, 1987.

———. "'The Scandal of the Cross': Atonement in the Pauline Corpus." In *The Glory of the Atonement: Essays in Honor of Roger Nicole*, edited by C. E. Hill and F. A. James III, 145–53. Downers Grove, IL: InterVarsity Press, 2004.

———. "Union with Christ: Some Biblical and Theological Reflections." In *Always Reforming: Explorations in Systematic Theology*, edited by A. T. B. McGowan, 271–88. Downers Grove, IL: IVP Academic, 2006.

———. "The Usefulness of the Cross." *Westminster Theological Journal* 41 (1978–79): 228–46.

Garlington, D. *In Defense of the New Perspective on Paul: Essays and Reviews.* Eugene, OR: Wipf and Stock, 2005, 1–28 ("The New Perspective on Paul: Two Decades On").

Lusk, R. "A Response to 'The Biblical Plan of Salvation.'" In *The Auburn Avenue Theology, Pros and Cons*, edited by E. C. Beisner, 118–48. Fort Lauderdale, FL: Knox Theological Seminary, 2004.

Luther, M. *Luther's Works,* vol. 35: *Word and Sacrament*, vol. 1. Edited by E. T. Bachmann. Philadelphia: Fortress Press, 1959.

Machen, J. G. *The New Testament: An Introduction to Its Literature and History.* Edited by W. J. Cook. Edinburgh: Banner of Truth, 1976.

———. *What Is Faith?* London: Hodder & Stoughton, 1925.

Mueller, J. T. *Christian Dogmatics.* St. Louis: Concordia, 1934.

Murray, J. *Collected Writings of John Murray*. Edited by I. Murray. 4 vols. Edinburgh: Banner of Truth, 1976–82.

———. *The Epistle to the Romans*. Grand Rapids: Eerdmans, 1959.

———. *Principles of Conduct: Aspects of Biblical Ethics*. Grand Rapids: Eerdmans, 1957.

———. *Redemption Accomplished and Applied*. Grand Rapids: Eerdmans, 1955.

Owen, J. *The Doctrine of Justification by Faith*, vol. 5 of *The Works of John Owen*. 1677. Edinburgh: Banner of Truth. 1965.

Pieper, F. *Christian Dogmatics*. St. Louis: Concordia, 1951, 1953.

Porter, S. E., and Stovell, B. M., eds. *Biblical Hermeneutics: Five Views*. Downers Grove, IL: IVP Academic, 2012.

Ridderbos, H. *Paul: An Outline of His Theology*. Translated by J. R. de Witt. Grand Rapids: Eerdmans, 1975.

———. "The Redemptive-Historical Character of Paul's Preaching." In *When the Time Had Fully Come: Studies in New Testament Theology*, 44–60. Grand Rapids: Eerdmans, 1957.

———. *Redemptive History and the New Testament Scriptures*. Translated by H. De Jongste. Revised by R. B. Gaffin, Jr. Phillipsburg, NJ: Presbyterian and Reformed, 1988.

———. "Terugblik en uitzicht." In *De dertiende apostel en het elfde gebod: Paulus in de loop der eeuwen*, edited by G. C. Berkouwer and H. A. Oberman, 189–97. Kampen: Kok, 1971.

Sanders, E. P. *Paul and Palestinian Judaism: A Comparison of Patterns of Religion*. London: SCM, 1977.

Schmid, H. *The Doctrinal Theology of the Evangelical Lutheran Church*. 3rd rev. ed. Minneapolis: Augsburg, 1961.

Schweitzer, A. *The Mysticism of Paul the Apostle*. Translated by W. Montgomery. New York: H. Holt, 1931.

Turretin, F. *Institutes of Elenctic Theology*. 1679. Translated by G. M. Giger. 3 vols. Phillipsburg, NJ: P&R, 1994.

VanDrunen, D. *Living in God's Two Kingdoms: A Biblical Vision for Christianity and Culture*. Wheaton, IL: Crossway, 2010.

Versteeg, J. P. *Adam in the New Testament: Mere Teaching Model or First Historical Man?* Translated by R. B. Gaffin Jr. 2nd ed. Phillipsburg, NJ: P&R, 2012.

Vos, G. *Biblical Theology: Old and New Testaments.* Grand Rapids: Eerdmans, 1948.

———. *The Pauline Eschatology.* 1930. Grand Rapids: Baker, 1979.

Warfield, B. B. *The Inspiration and Authority of the Bible.* Edited by Samuel G. Craig. Philadelphia: Presbyterian and Reformed, 1948.

Waters, G. *Justification and the New Perspectives on Paul: A Review and Response.* Phillipsburg, NJ: P&R, 2004.

Westerholm, S. *Perspectives Old and New on Paul: The "Lutheran" Paul and His Critics.* Grand Rapids: Eerdmans, 2004.

Whiteley, D. E. H. *The Theology of St. Paul.* Oxford: Blackwell, 1964.

Witsius, H. *The Economy of the Covenants between God and Man.* 1677. Translated by William Crookshank. 2 vols. Escondido, CA: Den Dulk Christian Foundation, 1990.

Wright, N. T. "The Letter to the Romans: Introduction, Commentary, and Reflections." In *The New Interpreter's Bible,* vol. 10. Nashville: Abingdon Press, 2002.

———. *The Resurrection of the Son of God*, vol. 3 of *Christian Origins and the Question of God.* London: SPCK, 2003.

———. *What Saint Paul Really Said.* Grand Rapids: Eerdmans, 1997.

Index of Scripture

Genesis
1:31—6
2—53
2:7—53n
3—53

Exodus
4:22—70
23:19—68

Leviticus
23:10-11—68

Deuteronomy
32:9—40

Job
34:11—109n

Psalm
62:12—108n
73:26—40
89:27—70
119:57—40

Proverbs
24:12—108n

Ecclesiastes
12:14—108n

Isaiah
25:8—102n7
53:5—40, 40n13
53:12—40
57:15—7

Jeremiah
10:16—40
17:10—109n
32:19—109n

Daniel
12:2—68

Hosea
13:14—102n7

Matthew
10:32—94n1
16:27—109
17:9—98
24:31—102
25:23—94n
25:33—94n

Luke
20:35—98

John
2:19—76n8

5:28-29—109-10
10:17-18—76n8

Acts
16:31—23, 116
17:31—107n
24:15—68

Romans—3, 51-52
1—38
1:1—25
1:2-4—116, 119
1:3-4—25
1:4—75
1:5—116, 116nn17-18, 119
1:16—51
1:17—116n19
1:18-20—33
1:18-32—34
1:18-3:20—36, 107, 108
1:19-21a—35
1:21-32—115
1:25—35
1:26-27—35
1:29-31—35
2:5—105, 108
2:5-11—108, 109, 110
2:5-13—109, 110
2:5-16—107
2:6—108, 111, 112
2:6-11—111
2:6-13—109
2:7—111
2:7-11—108
2:8—37, 105, 111
2:8-9—111
2:9—111
2:10—111
2:11—111
2:12-13—109, 110

2:13—93, 109
2:14-16—111n
2:16—109
2:29—108
3-4—95n3
3:9—36
3:19—36
3:20—35, 109
3:21—108, 109
3:23—36, 108
3:24-26—121
3:25—97
3:25-26—41, 103
4—119
4:7-8—55
4:24—98
4:25—25, 39, 40n12, 56, 74, 97
5—53
5:5-10—53
5:9—121
5:10—53
5:12-19—33, 36, 41
5:12-21—53, 54, 55-56, 104, 114
5:14—54
5:16-18—98, 99
5:18—56, 98, 100
5:18-19—121
5:19—93
5:21—98
6—72, 84
6-7—37, 87-88
6:2—80
6:2-7:6—71
6:4-5—71
6:6—37, 64
6:8—71
6:11—71
6:11-13—88
6:12—37, 80
6:12-13—83-85, 99

6:13—71
6:14—36, 37
6:16-20—37
6:22—37, 80
6:23—98
7:6—36
7:7-13—35
7:12—35, 36, 81
7:22—62
8:1—92
8:2—99
8:3—97
8:4—84
8:7—35
8:9—99
8:9-10—44
8:9-11—75, 111n
8:10—99-101, 99n
8:11—85
8:14—15
8:14-17—106
8:17—42, 45
8:18—104
8:18-23—48n
8:19—48, 48n, 106
8:21—48, 48n, 106
8:23—48n, 85, 104n8, 106
8:29—113, 114
8:30—122
8:31—120-21
8:32—121, 122
8:33—121
8:33-34—120-21, 122n
8:34—43, 121, 125
8:38-39—104, 105, 120, 122
10:4—36
10:9—22, 74
10:9-10—25
11—12
13:8-9—80

13:8-10—81
13:9—36
13:14—79
14:10—107n
16:7—42
16:25—116
16:26—116, 116nn17-18, 119

1 Corinthians
1:2—80
1:9—47, 48
1:13—41
1:18-23—38
1:18-3:22—25
1:30—58, 97, 122, 124
2:2—25
2:10—12
2:14—38
3:16-17—48
4:7—88
5:7—79
6:19—48
7:19—36, 81
11:7-9—34-35
12:3—25
12:13—48
15—44, 47, 53, 54, 67, 68, 102n6
15:1—27, 47
15:1-2—26
15:2—47
15:3—30, 40n12
15:3-4—26-34, 29, 38, 40
15:5—40n12
15:12-19—70
15:13—70
15:15—70
15:16—70
15:17—32
15:20—45, 67-70, 69n, 74, 77, 102
15:21-22—41, 53, 98

15:22—42
15:23—45, 68, 102
15:25-26—102
15:30—98
15:42-44—113
15:42-45—75
15:42-49—69, 73
15:44—73
15:44b-49—114
15:45—41, 44, 53n, 77, 85, 99
15:45-49—53
15:47—41, 53
15:49—104, 113, 114
15:50-52—102
15:54—102, 102n7
15:54-55—102, 103
15:54-56—101-2
15:55—102n7
15:56—102-3
15:57-58—103

2 Corinthians
1:22—85
3—44
3:6-11—36
3:17—44
3:18—114
4:4-6—64
4:7—64, 66, 84
4:10-11—104n9
4:16—61-62, 63-67, 64, 65, 66, 91, 92, 96, 99, 100
5:1-10—66, 107
5:2-4—104, 104n10
5:5—85
5:7—23, 66, 84, 105, 106-7
5:8—64, 104
5:10—107, 113
5:15—39
5:17—32

5:21—97
7:1—80
10:3—84
11:23-26—11
12:9-10—104n9
13:4—75n

Galatians—51, 51-52
1:1—30, 74
1:4—30-31, 32, 84
2:14—51
2:17—56
2:20—32, 45, 48, 58, 71, 77, 87, 99
3—95n3
3:17-25—36
3:27—79
3:28—64
4:4—42
5:1—79
5:2-6—112
5:5—93
5:6—112, 117, 118
5:19-21—35
5:22—80
5:25—79
6:7-9—110
6:14—25, 32
6:14-15—84
6:15—32

Ephesians—52
1:4—42, 45
1:9—42
1:13—49, 51
1:14—85
1:21—31
2:1—37, 47, 71
2:1-10—71-72
2:2—37
2:3—37, 42, 105

2:3-4—38
2:5—37, 47, 71
2:5-6—71, 76n9
2:8-9—52, 88, 115-16
2:10—71, 88, 115-16, 117
3:16—62
3:16-17—44
3:17—47
4:17-19—34
4:19—35
4:22-24—79-80
5:6—37
5:8—79
5:32—43
6:2-3—81
6:12—73

Philippians
1:6—77, 80, 86
1:21—103
1:23—64, 103
1:29—104n9
2:6-11—25
2:8—33, 97
2:12-13—83
2:13—88
3:3—108
3:8-9—56
3:10—104n9
3:11—98
3:21—114

Colossians
1:13—31-32, 51
1:15—114
1:15-18—53
1:18—70
1:18-19—123
1:23—124
1:24-29—123

1:26—123
1:27—45, 123, 125
2—72
2:9—123
2:12—71
2:12-13—71
2:13—37
3:1—71, 76n9, 78-79, 79n, 84
3:1-4—71, 77-79
3:2—78, 78n
3:3—78
3:4—45, 99
3:6—37
3:9-10—64, 79

1 Thessalonians
1:3—117
1:9-10—15-16
1:10—37
2:13—9
4:6—48
4:8—48
4:13-14—22
4:14—74, 74n, 104, 104n8
4:14-18—68
4:16—74, 74n, 102
5:23—80

2 Thessalonians
1:6—37
1:8-9—37, 105
1:11—117
2:1-12—13
2:6—13
2:10—37
2:12—37
3:1-2—22

1 Timothy
1:12-16—87

1:13—48
1:15—33, 48
3:16—97

2 Timothy
1:9—52
2:8—25
3:16—9, 9n
4:1—107n
4:8—93

Titus
3:5-7—52,
115

Hebrews
1:1-2a—7-8
12:14—80

James
2:18—87, 117,
118
2:21-24—118-19

1 Peter
1:3—98

2 Peter
1:21—15
3:16—11-12, 14

1 John
3:2—107

Revelation
20:13—110
22:12—110

Index of Subjects and Names

Adam
  and Christ, 33, 41, 44, 44n, 53–54, 75, 76, 115
  as first human being, 33, 33n
  sin and death of, 33, 37n11, 104
adoption, 21n1, 39, 93, 105–7
Allert, C. D., 9n
anthropology, 61–67, 76, 91, 92, 96, 99, 101
  image of God, 7, 34–35, 104–5, 114–15
  inner man/inner self, 62–67, 76–77, 99–101, 103
  outer man/outer self, 62–67, 99–102, 105, 107

Baur, F. C., 14, 14n, 28
Bavinck, H., 23n
Berkouwer, G. C., 88n16
biblical theology, 5, 6–10, 17–19
  covenant history, 5, 7, 54
  God's self-revelation: word and deed, 6–8
  history of redemption, 6, 15
  history of revelation, 7, 10
  "last days," 8
  natural revelation, 7, 36
  preredemptive special revelation, 7, 7n
  redemptive-historical, 5, 6–7, 10, 15–17, 21, 28, 29, 78, 123

relationship to systematic theology, 17–19
  salvation-historical, 4
Bultmann, R., 81

Calvin, John, 5, 25–26, 26n, 47n, 50, 50n23, 57n28, 59, 59nn29–30, 120, 120n
Campbell, C. R., 41n14
Christology, 33, 34
  Christ and Holy Spirit, 44, 44n, 75, 99
  death and resurrection of Christ, 15, 16, 25–28, 29, 30, 33–34, 38–39, 45, 47, 48, 61, 88, 123
  "firstborn from the dead," 70, 75, 123
  "firstfruits," 67–70, 75, 102
  states of humiliation and exaltation, 27
  two natures of Christ, 44, 76
  See also resurrection, of Christ
corporate and ecclesiological, 3, 23, 31, 34, 47–48, 51, 55, 56, 124
  Jew and Gentile, 3, 51, 54–55, 115
cosmic, 31, 48, 48n

Dabney, R. L., 95n2
death
  of Christ, 58, 103, 121 (see also Christology)

of human beings, 37, 96–105
as penal, 37, 37n11, 98–105
of Christ, 58, 103, 121 (see also
Christology)
Dunn, J. D. G., 1n, 2, 2n, 37n10

eschatology, 29–30, 61–67, 67–77,
85–86, 91–93, 123
age to come, 69, 84
already/not yet (two-age construct), 30–32, 65–66, 72, 78,
84–85, 91–93, 96, 99–101,
106–7, 112, 120–22
new creation, 32, 69
present age, 30–32, 65, 84

faith, 21n1, 22–23, 29, 47–48, 61, 64,
65, 66, 71, 82, 88–89, 95, 96,
100, 101, 107–14, 114–22
"obedience of faith," 116–17, 116n18
final judgment, 94, 101, 107–14
"according to works,"107–12, 113,
114–19 (see also sanctification)
Fisher, J., 95n2
Flavel, J., 95n2

Gaffin, Richard B., Jr., 8n9, 34n,
44n, 45n17, 97n, 104n9,
116n18, 122n
Garlington, D., 1n, 116n18
God
aseity of, 7
Creator-creature relationship, 7,
35, 36
incomprehensibility of, 12
as triune, 40
wrath of, 28, 37, 41, 42, 105 (see
also death as penal)
gospel, 3, 4, 25, 27, 39–40, 47, 49, 51,
64, 81, 86, 109, 117, 124

See also Christology, death and
resurrection of Christ

Heidelberg Catechism, 85–86
historia salutis (history of salvation),
4–5, 21, 21n2, 22, 27–29, 72,
123
salvation accomplished, 3–4, 21,
23, 29, 72

justification, 2–4, 5, 21n1, 27–29,
39, 43, 45–46, 48, 49, 49n22,
50–59, 86, 87, 88, 91–122
the eschatological "already" of,
91–92
by faith, 28, 51–52, 82, 109, 111,
114, 119 (see also faith)
forensic (judicial), 28, 45–46,
50, 55–56, 67, 91, 93, 94, 96,
97–107, 113, 120–22
future aspect of, 91–114
imputation of righteousness, 56,
57–59, 97, 111, 114, 121, 122, 124
and intercession of Christ, 121–22,
125
"life," 55–56, 98
and resurrection of Christ, 56,
96–99, 121
righteousness, 55–56, 58–59,
97–100, 114, 121, 122, 124, 125
and union with Christ, 45–46,
56–59, 91, 124

kingdom proclamation of Jesus, 29

law of God, 35–36, 81
law-gospel antithesis, 114–18
Lusk, R., 57n27
Luther, Martin, 22, 57n25, 92, 119,
119n

Machen, J. Gresham, 118, 118nn20–22

Marcion, 11, 19

metaphor, 24, 46, 56, 68, 76–77, 76n9, 102

Montefiore, G. W., 2

Moore, G. F., 2

Mueller, J. T., 57n25

Murray, John, 45n17, 87n15, 99n, 110, 110n, 112n

ordo salutis (order of salvation), 3–5, 19, 21–23, 21nn1–2, 27–30, 33, 42–43, 49, 49n22, 61–62, 65, 72, 95n3, 123, 125
  individual, 3–4, 19, 21, 31, 48, 51, 56
  salvation applied, 3–4, 21, 29, 72

Overbeck, Franz, 11

Owen, J., 95n2

Pastoral Epistles, 52

Paul
  the apostle, 8–15, 15n
  epistemology of, 25
  and James, 118–19
  Saul, the Pharisee, 2–3, 34
  the theologian, 5–16, 17, 40, 80
  theology of, 4, 5, 10, 12–15, 23–34, 40, 47–48, 49, 54, 59

Pauline interpretation, 10–11, 18
  center of his theology, 23–59
  confessional Protestantism, 2
  Enlightenment, 28
  "good and necessary conse-quence," 13, 16–17, 96
  historical-critical, 17–18, 28–29, 94
  Lutheran, 21n1, 57, 57n25, 95n2
  modern, 9

New Perspective on Paul, 1–5, 18, 47–48, 51, 52, 54, 94, 115, 124

postmodern, 9

Reformation, 2–3, 5, 18, 21n1, 28–29, 39–40, 51, 56–57, 85–87, 91, 94–95, 123–24

Reformed, 57, 95n2

Reformers, 39, 49, 92

Roman Catholicism (Rome), 28, 92

Paul's letters
  canonical context of, 10, 15, 18–19
  clarity of, 10, 14
  difficulty of, 10–14
  "occasional" nature of, 6, 12–14, 24
  "Spirit-borne," 15
  thirteen, 10
  Word of God, 9–10, 12

Pelagian, 115

Pieper, F., 57n25

resurrection
  of Christ, 67–77, 96–97, 98, 102–3, 121, 123 (*see also* Christology)
  future bodily, of believers, 23, 48n, 64, 66, 67–70, 72, 73–74, 77, 85, 92, 96, 101–3, 104–5, 106–7, 112–14
  future bodily, of unbelievers, 68
  harvest, 68–69, 72, 102
  present, of believers, 70–74, 76–77, 77–86, 88–89, 91–92, 99

reward, 110

Ridderbos, Herman, 5, 5n, 11, 11n13, 15n, 21, 21n2, 63n3, 82, 82n, 112n

sanctification, 29, 39, 43, 46, 49,
  49n22, 50, 67–89, 91, 96, 114,
  124
  definitive sanctification, 87–88,
    87n15
  good works, 86–89
  indicative and imperative,
    77–85, 82n
  renovative, 46, 50, 67, 96
  See also resurrection, present, of
    believers
Sanders, E. P., 2, 45, 45n18
Schmid, H., 57n25
Schweitzer, Albert, 8, 8n10, 11, 11n12,
  28, 46, 46n
Scripture, 36
  content and form of, 9
  God-breathed, 9n, 15, 18
  God the primary author of, 17
  revelatory word, 9
  theological method, 16
  See also Paul, the apostle; biblical
    theology
Second Temple Judaism, 2, 9, 31,
  31n, 34
semi-Pelagian, 115
sin, 32–34, 34–40
  enslaving and corrupting power
    of, 28–29, 32, 37, 38–39, 46, 47,
    67
  guilt of, 32, 36, 38–39, 46, 47, 55,
    67
  illegal, 35–36
  plight of and solution for, 33–34,
    38
  relational, 34–35
  universal, 36–37, 107–8
  See also death as penal
soteriology, 3, 4, 5, 33, 34, 41, 45, 49–50,
  51–52, 55, 61, 66, 91, 93, 95, 96

Stendahl, Krister, 2
suffering of believers, 104
systematic theology, 16, 17–19

Tertullian, 19
timeless, 3, 3n4, 54, 78
Turretin, F., 95n2

union with Christ, 32, 40–46,
  41n14, 47–50, 49n22, 57, 61,
  64–67, 67–84, 88, 91, 95,
  96–98, 100, 103–4, 112, 113,
  119, 122, 124–25
  covenantal bond, 40–41
  existential, 42–45, 71–72
  indissoluble, 45
  mystical, 43
  "now and not yet" structure of,
    65–67
  predestinarian, 42, 45
  redemptive-historical, 42, 71
  representative, 43
  spiritual, 43–45
  See also adoption; justification;
    sanctification

VanDrunen, D., 48n
Versteeg, J. P., 33n, 38n
von Harnack, Adolf, 11
Vos, Geerhardus, 5, 5n, 6n, 7n8, 8,
  8n10, 13, 13n, 31n, 69n, 104n10

Warfield, B. B., 9n
Waters, G., 1n
Weiss, Johannes, 67
Westerholm, S., 1n
Westminster Confession of Faith,
  13, 16, 112, 114, 119, 120
Westminster Larger Catechism, 57,
  87n14, 94, 94n, 104n8, 113

Westminster Shorter Catechism, 35, 57n26, 87n14, 94, 94n, 104n8, 113

Westminster Standards, 93–95, 112–13

Westminster Standards subscription vows, 16n

Whiteley, D. E. H., 37n10

Witsius, H., 95n2

works of believers, 86–89, 107–112, 113, 114–19

"works of the law," 52, 54, 109, 115
  See also sanctification; final judgment

Wright, N. T., 2, 3, 3nn3–4, 4, 22n4, 73n, 76n9, 111n, 116n19